D1015580

••••••••••••••••

How to understand other people

How to make them like you

How to get them to do just
what you want!

How to get power through
People Watching

ALSO BY VERNON COLEMAN

The Medicine Men (1975)
Paper Doctors (1976)
Everything You Want to Know About
    Ageing (1976)
Stress Control (1978)
The Home Pharmacy (1980)
Aspirin or Ambulance (1980)
Face Values (1981)
Guilt (1982)
The Good Medicine Guide (1982)
Stress and Your Stomach (1983)
Bodypower (1983)
Thomas Winsden's Cricketing
    Almanack (1983)
A Guide to Child Health (1984)
An A to Z of Women's Problems
    (1984)
Bodysense (1984)
Taking Care of Your Skin (1984)
Diary of a Cricket Lover (1984)
Life Without Tranquillisers (1985)
High Blood Pressure (1985)
Diabetes (1985)
Arthritis (1985)
Eczema and Dermatitis (1985)
The Story of Medicine (1985)
Natural Pain Control (1986)
Mindpower (1986)
Addicts and Addictions (1986)
Dr Vernon Coleman's Guide to
    Alternative Medicine (1988)
Stress Management Techniques (1988)
Overcoming Stress (1988)
Know Yourself (1988)
The Health Scandal (1988)
The 20 Minute Health Check (1989)
Sex for Everyone (1989)
Mind Over Body (1989)
Eat Green Lose Weight (1990)
Toxic Stress (1991)
Why Animal Experiments Must Stop
    (1991)
The Drugs Myth (1992)

Arthritis (1993)
Backache (1993)
Stress and Relaxation (1993)
Complete Guide to Good Sex (1993)
Why Doctors Do More Harm Than
    Good (1993)
Betrayal of Trust (1994)
Know Your Drugs (1994)
Food for Thought (1994)
The Traditional Home Doctor (1994)
I Hope Your Penis Shrivels Up (1994)

Novels
The Village Cricket Tour (1990)
The Bilbury Chronicles (1992)
Bilbury Grange (1993)
Mrs Caldicot's Cabbage War (1993)
The Man Who Inherited a Golf
    Course (1993)
The Bilbury Revels (1994)
Deadline (1994)
Bilbury Pie (1994)

Writing as Edward Vernon
Practice Makes Perfect (novel, 1977)
Practise What You Preach (novel,
    1978)
Getting into Practice (novel, 1979)
Aphrodisiacs—An Owner's Manual
    (1983)
The Complete Guide to Life (1984)

As Marc Charbonnier
Tunnel (novel, 1980)

With Dr Alan C. Turin
No More Headaches (1981)

With Alice
Alice's Diary (1989)
Alice's Adventures (1992)

People Watching

by the author of
Know Yourself

Vernon Coleman

BLUE
BOOKS

Published by the European Medical Journal. (First published in 1995
by Blue Books), Publishing House, Trinity Place, Barnstaple, Devon,
EX32 9HJ, England

Reprinted 1995, 1996

ISBN 1 898947 73 2

A catalogue record for this book is available from the British Library

Printed and bound in England by Biddles Ltd, Guildford and King's Lynn

Contents

• • • • • • • • • •

Author's Note

● ● ● ● ● ● ● ● ● ● ● ● ● ● ● ●

Most of this book applies to women as much as to men. But to simplify the text I have used 'he' and 'him' throughout – rather than cluttering things up by constantly offering 'she' and 'her' as alternatives.

Introduction

· · · · · · · · · · · ·

Have you ever envied Sherlock Holmes his remarkable powers of observation? Have you ever wished that you could sum up people as quickly and as accurately

Well, learning to judge people isn't as difficult as you might think. You simply need to know what to look for – and what conclusions to draw from the way people dress and behave. The colour of a man's shirt can tell you a great deal about him. The sort of handbag a woman carries can speak volumes about her personality. The way a man holds his head when he talks will tell you as much about him as the way his partner sits tells you about her.

People Watching is just about the only hobby I know of that costs nothing, isn't uncomfortable or painful, doesn't put you at risk, is both entertaining and educational and can be enjoyed alone or in company.

If you ever travel by train, tube, bus or aeroplane; if you ever spend time sitting in waiting rooms or standing in queues; or if you ever have an hour to kill at an airport or railway station, then you really should take up People Watching

By People Watching I don't just mean staring idly around you, of course. We all do that all the time. There is as much difference between that and proper People Watching as there is between running for a bus and taking part in an international athletics meeting!

The chances are that in the past you have limited yourself to watching the truly unusual and clearly exceptional individuals who stood out from the crowd because of some bizarre eccentricity.

You'll have noticed the fellow with the mohican hair style dyed green. And you'll have seen the girl with the shaven head and no shoes.

But they were probably the least interesting people around!

Once you know what you're looking for, you can look around you in a crowd and tell a great deal about the people you see simply by looking at their clothes, their accessories and their luggage. You have to be careful, of course. You have to learn not to jump to conclusions but to use all the information that is available before making a judgement. Quick, instant assessments can be way off the mark but by carefully analysing all the evidence you can build up pen portraits of the people you see which are uncannily accurate. Moreover you can also make accurate judgements about their relationships with the people with whom they are travelling.

But People Watching isn't just entertaining; isn't just a pleasant way to spend a few otherwise idle moments.

If you study this book carefully, and learn to practise People Watching with care and thought, then you will find that you can learn many things that will help you in your own life. You can learn how to 'read' people whom you meet socially and in business. You can learn how to project the right image, how to make a good impression on the people you meet, how to make people like you, how to manipulate strangers, how to outwit competitors and how to enjoy a better sex life.

What more can you expect from a book?

Try People Watching. I think you'll enjoy it.

Vernon Coleman, Devon 1994

PART 1

Understanding
People

● ● ● ● ● ● ● ● ● ● ● ● ● ●

WE TALK NOT just with our mouths but with our eyes, our hands and our bodies. Between us we use about a million different non verbal cues and signals – some of them inherited, some of them cultural and some learned. These non verbal signals are so important that an astonishing ninety per cent of the messages we want to get across to other people are carried in the way we move, sit, walk and speak.

Gestures and body language

The average sentence takes less than three seconds to speak and the average person speaks for no more than about ten minutes a day – for the rest of the time we talk with our bodies. Words are used to transmit information but we use non verbal methods of communication to transmit our attitudes, emotions and feelings.

Strangely, however, although our lives and destinies are dominated by our physical actions and reactions most of us remain blissfully unaware of just how much our posture, movements and gestures are giving away what we really think.

We should take body language more seriously. The evidence shows that when our bodies are saying something different from our mouths it is our bodies which are telling the truth!

Some non verbal cues are universal and easy to 'read'. When we are happy we smile; when we are unhappy we frown; when we agree we nod our heads; when we disagree we shake our heads – and when we don't understand we shrug our shoulders.

We use the two finger salute to express anger, fury or distaste; we use the thumbs up gesture to signify approval, agreement or contentment and when we want to show our agreement we make a ring with our finger and thumb.

But most non verbal gestures are more subtle than these. Here is my analysis of how we use everyday gestures to say what we are really thinking!

Courtship gestures (female)

When a woman sees a man whose attention she wants to attract she will:

* stand with her legs slightly apart

* stand as erect as she can – holding in her stomach

* touch her hair – and maybe take out a mirror, comb and lipstick

* roll her lips and open her mouth very slightly

* sit or stand with her foot or knee pointing at the man she is interested in

* speak in an unusually low voice

* touch herself repeatedly – for example, stroking her thigh

* if sitting she may cross and uncross her legs repeatedly – showing slightly more leg each time she does so

* slip her foot in and out of her shoe

* glance shyly at him from under her eyelids

* expose her wrists in his direction

* toss her head – particularly if she has long hair which she can toss out of her eyes

❋ repeatedly fondle some phallic object such as a wine glass stem, cigarette, cigarette lighter or pen

Courtship gestures (male)

When a man sees a woman whom he fancies – and wants to impress – he will make a number of automatic adjustments to the way he sits, stands or moves. (Incidentally, although these gestures and body movements may seem sexy, masculine and attractive to a woman they are likely to seem aggressive, insincere and arrogant if seen by a man.) The courting male will:

❋ stand very erect, holding in his stomach so that he appears as thin as possible

❋ straighten his tie and, if possible, check the knot in a mirror

❋ comb his hair or pat it with his fingers – and, if possible, check his hair in a nearby mirror

❋ stand with his body facing the woman he fancies – with at least one foot pointing directly towards her

❋ sit with his legs wide apart

❋ try to catch her gaze – and then look directly into her eyes

❋ stand with his hands on his hips or his thumb tucked into his belt.

Feeling critical

Someone you are talking to may say that he agrees with you but you can tell that he feels critical (and is only saying that he agrees with you to be nice) if:

❋ he rests his chin on his thumb or fist with a finger

pointing up the side of his cheek

* repeatedly rubs at the back of his neck
* he folds his arms while listening to you
* clenches his fists while listening to you
* holds his head down
* picks imaginary bits of fluff off his clothes

Liars and lying

When children lie they tend to use their hands to cover up their mouths. As we get older we become rather more subtle about this. The adult liar will put his hand to his face – maybe touching his nose or eye – but won't necessarily touch his mouth. People who are telling untruths may also:

* pull at their collars or play with a necklace
* put a finger, pen or pencil into their mouths
* look at the ceiling or the floor

People will often cover up their ears when they are hearing something they don't want to listen to – and they will cover (or partly cover) their eyes when they think they are going to see something they don't want to see.

Fighting talk

Someone who is angry or feeling particularly determined will:

* lean forward when talking
* make a fist with his dominant hand
* jab a pointing finger in the direction of the person he is addressing
* make karate chop movements with his hand

❊ take off his jacket and roll up his sleeves

An aggressive individual will hold his hands in such a way that the palms are hidden. When shaking hands such a dominant, forceful individual will hold out a hand with the palm slightly hidden, pointing slightly downwards.

Meek, submissive

Gentle, honest, self effacing people who want help, support or guidance will stand with their hands held in such a way that their palms are showing. When they shake hands the hand they offer will be held out palm up.

Nervousness

When we are nervous or anxious we give away our feelings in many different ways. We are, for example, likely to:

❊ hold something in front of us – a handbag, book, magazine, briefcase or bunch of flowers. At a party the nervous individual will hold a plate or a glass of wine with both hands – rather as though holding a shield

❊ play with a watch strap, cuff link or piece of jewellery; psychiatrists often say that a woman who has an unhappy marriage will play incessantly with her wedding ring (now that more men are wearing wedding rings the same is probably true of men too)

❊ twist a handkerchief in our fingers

❊ play with a pen or pencil or paperclip (in doctors' waiting rooms and radio studios you can usually see several broken paperclips and torn up paper tissues on the floor)

❊ doodle endlessly on any handy piece of paper

❊ sit with legs crossed tightly

❋ hold hands with ourselves – in front of our bodies

❋ stand with ankles crossed

Bored and impatient

People who are bored will use a hand to support their head.

When we're impatient we tend to tap our feet or drum our fingers on the table. The faster our feet tap (or our fingers drum) the more impatient we are. Someone who wants you to stop talking may:

❋ change his posture

❋ take off his spectacles

❋ start playing with a pen or some other object

❋ swivel or move his chair so that his position is changed

❋ break eye contact

❋ suddenly sit forwards

Confident and arrogant

People who are full of confidence will:

❋ sit astride a chair with the back of the chair in front of them and their arms resting on it

❋ sit with both hands clasped behind their head

❋ make both hands into a steeple

❋ walk with hands clasped behind their back

❋ stare straight at the middle of your face when talking to you

❋ sit with legs crossed very loosely – with, for example, one ankle resting on the other knee

Note

It is important to remember to make your assessment of

any individual not on the basis of a single gesture, movement or position but on the basis of a number of gestures and movements.

You should no more attempt to judge an individual on the basis of a single gesture than you would be prepared to judge an individual on the basis of the first word you heard him utter.

Territories

All creatures have territories. A domestic cat will fight if a cat from a neighbouring garden wanders onto its territory. A robin will make a terrific fuss if another robin strays into its adopted space. In the wild animals will kill intruders who dare to move into the land they consider to be their own.

Human beings are just the same.

Try, for example, walking into a stranger's garden and sitting down on the grass. You aren't doing any harm but you will arouse a great sense of anger in the house-owner. Or try walking into someone else's office when he or she isn't there. You'll feel a strange sense of guilt as you enter. You'll feel as though you are intruding or trespassing. Or, next time you visit a friend's home try sitting in the chair in which your host normally sits. You'll soon notice that he becomes edgy and uncomfortable. He'll probably deny that he doesn't like you sitting in his chair but he will find it difficult to settle and he will be easily irritated.

In addition to our territorial boundaries and feelings of 'ownership' over physically defined areas (homes, cars, offices, chairs etc.) we also have fairly clearly defined personal spaces and we get very upset when other people break the unwritten rules and enter, uninvited, into our personal spaces.

So, for example, if you're sitting in an almost empty train and a stranger comes and sits right next to you then the chances are that you will feel threatened, offended and uncomfortable. If you are sitting in an almost empty cinema and a stranger comes and chooses to sit just three seats away from you then you will feel edgy and irritated by his presence – harmless though it may be.

In ordinary everyday encounters we have three categories of personal space.

First, there is the 'social space'. When we stand in a shop or talk to a workman or have a conversation with a stranger we like to keep a distance of at least four feet between us and them. Under some circumstances the 'social space' can be greater than this – it is hardly ever any less.

Next, there is the 'personal space'. When we talk to people we know well – business acquaintances, friends and so on – then we allow them to come much closer to us. We can feel comfortable even if they are just a foot or so away from us.

Finally, we have an 'intimate space' – the space that is less than a foot away from us. We only allow those who are really close to us – lovers and closest relatives – to enter this very personal space.

If anyone steps over the imaginary line and enters the wrong zone, we feel desperately uncomfortable. We usually move backwards or, if that isn't possible, lean backwards. If a salesman moves too close we feel offended and we want to get away from him as soon as possible. If a stranger at a party pushes into our 'intimate space' we mumble excuses and move away.

When we are forced to allow strangers into our 'personal space' and even our 'intimate space' (as, for example, often happens on trains or lifts) then we do everything we can to make it clear that the situation is an abnormal one which we are accepting under sufferance. We read our newspaper or magazine, we avoid eye contact, we show no emotion, we keep very still and we do not talk.

The existence of these different spaces can often lead to confusion. For example, if you start a job in a new office you will probably find that your colleagues will wander in and out of one another's personal spaces. But you will be expected to keep your distance – in your social space – until you are properly accepted. It is worth remembering, too, that in some parts of the world these spaces can vary. In the country, for example, social, personal and intimate spaces tend to be much larger than they are in towns or cities. Country folk often prefer to wave a greeting rather than move close enough to shake hands.

It is also possible to cause great offence without meaning to by the way you act in public places. For example, if you walk into an almost empty cloakroom where there are just two other people hanging up their coats you can offend them both by choosing a peg that is too close to one and too far away from the other. Both will feel most comfortable if you choose a peg that is equidistant – preferably right in the middle.

Territories are, undoubtedly, guarded jealously and there are many fine rules governing behaviour. It is even possible to define a relationship fairly accurately by watching the behaviour of the individuals concerned. So, for example, when two people kiss, if their hips touch they are (or are likely to become) lovers. On the other hand if a space is visible at hip level then they are either 'just good friends' or else they are consciously making an effort to appear 'just good friends'. If one individual leans forward for the kiss while the other leans backwards then you can see which one of the two is more enthusiastic about the act of kissing.

In order to maintain the sanctity of their territories many individuals use pieces of furniture and social rituals to protect themselves and preserve their 'rights'. Later in this book I will explain exactly how you can use objects and rituals to manipulate other people's feelings and to manage your relationships with others.

Clothes

You can tell an awful lot about someone by the clothes he or she wears. (Though you must, of course, remember that if you're going to judge people who have to wear a uniform when they are at work – or who have to wear clothes of a particular style or colour – then you must wait until you can see them in the sort of clothes they choose to wear when they are not working).

The classical conformist, the person who chooses to wear chain store clothes in subdued colours, is making a statement just as clearly and distinctively as the individual who deliberately chooses unconventional clothes. The conformist is telling you that he wants to be seen as one of the crowd, as 'average' and 'middle of the road'. He doesn't want to be seen as different or perceived as any sort of threat. The unconventional individual, on the other hand, is keen to tell you that he is special, unique, creative and 'one in a million'.

Of course, neither of these extremes are necessarily what they seem to be and you must always take care to consider an individual as part of his surroundings. Never make judgements based on a glimpse or on a view of an individual on his own.

A youth who wears bright green trousers, a violent orange shirt, nailed boots and rings in his nose and both ears may seem at first sight to be a committed individual who is determined to be seen as an aggressive non conformist. However, if that youth belongs to a gang of twenty or thirty youths who all wear bright green trousers, violent orange shirts and nailed boots then it suddenly becomes clear that he isn't quite so much of an individual after all. Indeed, he may be more determined to fit in with his surroundings and less prepared to stand out from the crowd than the gang member who insists on wearing a sober grey suit, a white shirt and a striped tie.

And remember too that many individuals who have to wear clothes of a particular type in order to do their jobs effectively often stamp their personalities on their appearance by wearing brightly coloured socks, ties, belts or braces. The sober suited businessman who wears bright red socks and bright red braces may well be a more aggressive and more unusual individual than the gang member who has his hair styled with blue paint and super glue.

Finally, remember that the type of clothing an individual chooses to wear may reflect personal mood changes. Someone who suddenly starts to wear black all the time may be suffering from a persistent and deep depression.

General signs

Here are some general guidelines about clothing

❉ Someone who invariably wears formal, bespoke, expensive suits, handmade shoes and silk, monogrammed shirts isn't just conservative and wealthy – he also wants you to know that he is conservative and wealthy.

❉ Army surplus clothing, overalls, boiler suits and denim suits suggest an 'up the workers' image – particularly if the clothes are decorated with political slogans. It is dangerous to try and guess how wealthy someone is if they dress like this.

❋ Neat, well tailored clothes in bold stripes (and with accessories in bold colours) suggest a businesslike, aggressive approach.

❋ An image that looks unstructured, contains lots of woollen items and is noticeable for floral patterns and pastel colours suggests a caring, relaxed attitude and someone who is gentle and friendly.

❋ A classic grey suit suggests reliability, punctuality and honesty.

❋ Anything truly fashionable suggests a trendy, progressive outlook – particularly if the person wearing it usually seems to follow the latest fashions.

❋ Loose, crumpled clothes, generally untidy, with the pockets bulging, suggests an intellectual, thoughtful approach to life.

❋ A body hugging dress, a track suit, a pair of shorts and a T shirt or a leotard and a skirt suggest a fit, sensual, natural, health loving, 'physical' sort of person.

❋ People who generally chooses to wear natural fibres (such as silk, satin, mohair or cashmere) enjoy tactile sensations – this is particularly true if the individual concerned is frequently seen to stroke or touch fabrics and materials. Such a 'tactile' individual will often rub his fingers over his body in order to get rid of any wrinkles that may have developed in the material.

❋ Individuals who choose to wear quiet, sober, respectable clothing on a night out (for him: dark suit, white shirt, sober tie, lace up shoes – for her: knee length skirt, high necked blouse, flesh coloured tights, low heeled shoes, discreet make up and jewellery) tend to be cautious and respectable. Individuals who choose more outrageous clothes (for him: open neck satin shirt, tight trousers – for her: visible cleavage, very high heeled shoes, false eyelashes, heavy make up, mini skirt, hot pants, fun fur, sequins or anything lamé) are more likely to be socially and sexually aggressive and experimental.

❋ Apart from natural fibres (see above) you can tell something about people by the materials they choose to wear.

• people who are in a hurry tend to wear synthetics

• practical, down to earth, 'nature' loving people often choose cotton or linen

• coarse woven materials are chosen by people who want to protect themselves from the world

❋ A woman who usually prefers high necklines is probably anxious to be thought of as an individual rather than as a 'woman' or a thing of beauty. On the other hand a woman who regularly shows a daring amount of cleavage – and who draws attention to it with something bright and dangly around her neck – is probably very sure of her femininity and not above using her looks to help her get what she wants out of life. The amount of bosom a woman bares doesn't necessarily tell you how sexy she is – but it does tell you a great deal about her approach to life and the way she sees herself.

❋ A man who wears button down collars and/or uses a tie pin will probably be rather obsessive – and possibly sexually repressed. A man who wears a belt and braces is an uncertain pessimist lacking in confidence. A man who carries a neatly folded handkerchief in the breast pocket of his jacket will be rather vain and more than a little pompous. A man who has a neat row of pens or pencils visible in his outer breast pocket will be obsessional, cautious and meticulous.

He will also probably be rather dull and boring. But although he will be unimaginative he'll be hard working and reliable.

Shoes

You can tell quite a lot about an individual by the shoes he wears. A few years ago skilled hotel porters used to claim that it was much safer to judge a visitor's wealth and social status by the shoes he wore than by the cut or age of his clothes but these days I doubt if this simple trick is quite as reliable as it was. Here are some basic hints about footwear.

A woman who wears:

❊ high heeled, pointed shoes is likely to be keen to impress, sensitive to criticism but quick to criticise others. She is probably a sensual woman and a risk taker.

❊ flat shoes that are pointed and made of thin material is likely to be more worldly than most other women – she is probably rather cynical and suspicious. But she knows how to enjoy herself and is no stranger to fun.

❊ flat, square toed, sensible shoes is probably logical, reliable, practical and cautious.

A man who wears:

❊ well polished, well maintained leather shoes is keen to give a good impression. He is probably cautious, careful and reliable.

❊ sandals is probably relaxed, unambitious, unconcerned with worldly worries.

❊ pumps or trainers is impatient, impractical, unreliable and generally relaxed and calm.

❊ scruffy, down at heel leather shoes is unconcerned about his appearance, his image or the opinions of others. He is either a failure or an independent and successful man – too busy and too successful to worry about what other people think.

Accessories

You can tell a lot about people by the accessories they choose to wear or carry. Here are some fundamental People Watching facts.

Bags and briefcases

What people carry around with them can be a surprisingly reliable guide to their innermost thoughts.

For instance a woman who carries a tiny handbag enjoys being looked after and is probably unreliable. She is nearly always late for appointments. On the other hand a huge, capacious handbag suggests that a woman is independent, practical, reliable and punctual.

Similarly, you can find out a lot about a man by looking at the sort of case he carries with him to work.

A man who carries a black, composite attaché case is often stuck low down on the promotion ladder. Because he is unambitious, unimaginative and far, far too predictable he is likely to stay there.

A smart, mail order, modern, slim leather briefcase with brass fittings and a combination lock indicates someone who is ambitious and determined but probably still low down on the promotional ladder. If he has his initials on the case in gold then he is rather vain and pushy and perfectly prepared to step on the hands or heads of any competitors in his way.

An old, battered leather case with straps and buckles indicates a successful, experienced businessman who is confident and who has probably satisfied many (if not all) of his ambitions. Such a briefcase is carried by a man who no longer needs to make a good impression.

Jewellery

Here are some of the things you can learn from the jewellery people wear:

❊ a woman who wears a lot of rings is eager to be dominated by a man – and is quite likely to put up with all sorts of insults once she finds the strong, dominating man she needs.

❊ a woman who is forever playing with her wedding ring is struggling with an unhappy marriage.

❊ a woman who wears huge, bright ear rings is full of confidence, self assurance and ambition when she is with other people. By herself, at home, she is probably less sure of herself.

❊ a man who wears more than one ring is probably hen pecked – and happy to let a woman run his life for him.

Colours

There is increasing evidence to show that the colours we choose can tell others a great deal about the way we think, feel and are likely to act.

In America a growing number of employers are now using colour psychologists to help them choose new employees. Job applicants are given a collection of coloured cards and told to put the cards in order of preference. The psychologists then make assessments according to the applicants' choices. The results can make or break an individual's career. Someone who chooses red as their favourite colour will be regarded as full of vitality and energy. An applicant who chooses white will be regarded as an individual with little potential.

Not all psychologists use coloured cards to help them select suitable employees. Some experts study the colour of a candidate's clothes or the colour of the ink that he chooses to use on the application form. Use red ink, for example, and you'll be branded as aggressive, arrogant and pig headed. Prefer violet ink (Hitler's favourite colour when writing letters) and you'll be put down as a dominating type who is likely to find it difficult to obey instructions.

Clearly, the easiest way to use colour coding to assess the people you meet is to look at the clothes they choose to wear.

It is, of course, much easier to use colour coding to help assess women than it is to use the technique to assess men. In almost all walks of life women are allowed far more freedom when choosing clothes than men are. Few men would turn up at the office in bright red trousers or arrive at an evening function in a purple evening dress suit. Women, on the other hand, have the social freedom to select whatever colours they fancy.

There are however ways around this problem for even when he has to wear a sober suit to attend a business meeting there are many opportunities for the executive to express his personality. The choice of neck tie, braces, handkerchief and socks can all be extremely significant. And, of course, outside working hours it is much easier to learn something about a man's personality by looking at the clothes he has selected. (This is why so many employers like to meet prospective employees in a 'social' situation.)

When studying an individual's clothes it is important to remember that mood can have a very dramatic effect on the choice of clothing to be worn. Someone who feels particularly happy when shopping will often choose brighter colours than they would otherwise have selected. A woman who feels depressed while flicking through the available clothes in her wardrobe is likely to choose something dark to wear. A man who is feeling aggressive and dynamic may pick out a bright red tie.

Although important and easy to study clothes are not, of course, the only way to use colour to judge an individual's character. Everything an individual chooses – from the paint on his walls to the sheets on his bed – will tell you something about him.

The colour code

Note: when using the 'colour code' to assess personality and mood it is important to look for an overall dominant colour or to look for something which stands out as unusually expressive. Remember too that on the whole men tend to choose darker colours while women chose softer, pastel colours.

White :: innocence, purity, chastity and loyalty.

White suggests honesty, trustworthiness and a desire to be led or dominated. It also denotes an enthusiasm for old fashioned beliefs and ideals. When worn as a uniform white suggests aloofness and authority.

Yellow :: lonely, logical, cold and dictatorial.

Someone who chooses yellow probably has difficulty in expressing or communicating emotions. He may be unpredictable but will probably be knowledgeable. He will work hard in bursts of energy, will have great hopes for future happiness and will be desperate for release from emotional conflicts.

Green :: accurate, precise, clear, obsessive and consistent.

Green does suggest a sense of insecurity – people who choose this colour need plenty of reassurance. People who like green are usually peaceful and fair – they make good negotiators or arbitrators.

Blue:: relaxing, calm, orderly and neat.

People who like blue may seem cold and even frigid occasionally but are usually far more susceptible to emotional traumas than those around them may realise. Although the colour blue suggests relaxation it is often chosen, paradoxically, by those who find relaxation difficult. Superficially those who choose blue may seem balanced, secure and placid but that is probably something that they aspire to rather than something they regularly attain.

Red :: assertive, energetic, forceful, dangerous, sexy.

People who select red are often impulsive, with a great will to win, they want a full life, with intense experiences, they are creative, erotic and sensual. They have powerful physical appetites. They get angry easily and suffer from stress a lot. People who like red are natural leaders but they may find it difficult to concentrate or apply themselves to long-term projects. Their energy often results in unfaithfulness.

Brown :: shy, passive, reliable but dependable.

People who wear a lot of brown put great importance on 'home', 'stability' and 'security'. They enjoy material comforts. Sensuous contentment and physical ease are important to people who choose brown as a dominant colour. Illness, conflicts and other problems can cause a considerable amount of disturbance. People who wear brown have a deeply hidden sensitive nature.

Pink :: warm, compassionate, romantic.

People who like pink want to share their energies, emotions and feelings. They are generous, feminine and very alive. They have strong sexual feelings which may sometimes be repressed. They enjoy emotional involvements rather than physical intimacies. They enjoy being with other people. They want to share their lives and to give as well as to take. With the person they love people who wear pink can be very expressive – and sometimes surprisingly broad minded when it comes to experimenting with new methods of loving.

Orange :: a real mixture of emotions.

People who choose to wear orange are sometimes hyper-active, sometimes almost inactive. Confused and often confusing.

Purple and **Violet** :: mentally and emotionally insecure, immature and irresponsible.

People who love purple are often passionate, mysterious, spiritual and philosophical. They enjoy ceremony, tend to create great projects (and think 'big') but often turn out to be dreamers. They have wonderful ideas but rarely seem able to put their ideas into practice.

Grey :: anonymous, shy, self-effacing.

People who like grey find it difficult to commit themselves or become involved. They want to remain slightly distant from the rest of the world. They shield themselves from outside stimuli.

Beige :: indecisive, uncertain, wishy washy.

People who wear a lot of beige tend to find decision making difficult. They generally look for the easiest solution and prefer a compromise to a confrontation.

Black :: serious, gloomy, unhappy.

People who wear black outer clothing are often very serious, rather gloomy and maybe depressed – all this is particularly true if the clothing they wear is fulsome, long, loose or voluminous. Such individuals are often unhappy with the world. They may be anxious to change things. They are often full of secrets and they may wear black as an emotional and physical disguise. People who wear tight black outer clothing (e.g. a tight, short black skirt or a tight, low necked 'little black dress') may be beset with the same uncertainties and insecurities and may have the same natural sense of reticence but they may be covering up these fears with a sexually aggressive demeanour. Much the same is true of people (almost invariably women) who wear black underwear. They are usually beset with insecurity and a sense of instability. They wear black underwear to help themselves release their natural inhibitions. The black underwear makes them feel superficially sexy – it gives them confidence in themselves and their abilities. In black under-wear the shy and repressed individual can become an extrovert, becoming whatever the appropriate partner wants – for mutual pleasure. Black underwear enables the wearer to behave badly – despite a natural and otherwise crippling lack of confidence.

Homes

People say a great deal about themselves when they open their front doors. If you really want to know someone well try to get yourself invited into the place where they live. In a home the owner's personality breaks through all over the place – and cannot be easily disguised. It is possible to create a superficial veneer when away from home. But back in the 'nest' the truth is laid bare.

Cost does, of course, have a tremendous influence on the type of home people choose to live in. There aren't many poor people living in 30 bedroom castles and there aren't many millionaires living in single bedroom flats. But you can still discover a great deal about the personality of a home owner by looking at furnishings and other impedimenta.

Quick guide to home owners

1. The Intellectual Look

There are book shelves everywhere – and all the book shelves are filled with books. Most of the books are hard cover editions – very few of them are garish paperbacks, even fewer are bookclub editions. The home is rather untidy. There are rather scruffy, lumpy armchairs and the whole setting is time locked – no attempt has been made to keep up with fashions or styles. There are magazines, journals and piles of assorted papers everywhere. The owner of such a home will probably be intolerant and complacent and will be full of self-confidence.

2. The Hi–Tech Look

The furniture is for looking at rather than sitting on (or in). The lighting is complicated by dimmer switches and spot lights on rails. There is an open plan feel to the house. Everything is fitted – wardrobes, kitchen furniture etc. Most rooms are dominated by a piece of electrical equipment – a TV set, a video, a computer, a hi-fi. The owner of a Hi Tech Look house loves gadgets. There is probably a noise activated burglar alarm in the living room and an infra red heat detector activated security lighting system outside. The house provides living space – it certainly isn't a home. The owner likes clean, aseptic, unemotional relationships.

3. The Stockbroker Look

Comfort, style and solidity are the essentials. But the emphasis is on appearances rather than genuine pleasures – many of the things you see are 'fake'. The beams aren't real, the fireplace doesn't really work and the logs which appear to be burning are in reality a modern gas fire. There are family photographs in silver frames on top of the piano and the kitchen is full of complicated equipment. There are fitted carpets everywhere and the windows are draught-proofed and double glazed. The owner of such a property cares far more about appearances than about real life – he will gladly be seen to run a charity bazaar in his garden for the local mental hospital but he would fight tooth and nail if there were suggestions that the house next door be converted into a hostel for the mentally handicapped. Self centred and consistently selfish the owner has few genuine emotions left.

4. The Fogey Look

Everything in the house is a genuine antique – including the owners. Furniture, ornaments and pictures are all traditional and considerably out of date. Much the same can be said for the owners' opinions and attitudes.

5. Twentieth-Century Suburban

There are net curtains at the windows and heavily patterned carpets on the floor (the whole house is strictly functional and swirly, patterned carpets don't show the dirt as much as plain ones). The three piece suite has washable fitted covers on it and the book cases are packed with glass and china ornaments, mementoes and bric à brac. The furniture in the main living room is arranged around the TV set which is given pride of place in the room – rather like an altar at which the owner and his family worship daily. The owners of such a home are pragmatic and practical. They regard the horrors of the world as outside and beyond their control and take little interest in politics of any kind. However, when things which affect them directly go wrong they protest indignantly. In large cities there are fashionable variations on 'Twentieth-Century Suburban'. In smarter homes and flats the ornaments will be better made and more expensive and the net curtains will be replaced by tall plants in large nineteenth-century vases but the attitudes of the owners will be identical.

Around the home

🏠 Rich people tend to choose quieter colours than people less well off. If you are successful you don't need to make a statement when you have your home decorated.

🏠 Rich people often put up with shabby décor. The furnishings, carpets, curtains and furniture may be expensive but old and battered.

🏠 People who choose lots of patterned, floral wallpaper, curtains and chair coverings are often rather old fashioned and keen on 'natural' things.

🏠 Bedrooms are usually decorated by women. If you want to see a woman's taste (and test her personality) look at the bedroom where she normally sleeps.

🏠 Stripped pine and varnished wood are usually chosen by people who would love to live in the country but who usually live in the town.

🏠 Self-conscious individuals usually have a very smart (and brightly painted) front door and hallway – those are the parts of the house that are usually seen first.

🏠 Idealists – people with a strong sense of moral values – usually choose white walls, stripped pine and clean, simple, well made traditional style furniture.

People who chose very bright colours in their homes – either for walls or for furnishings or for furniture – need plenty of stimulation. Reds and pinks are favourite colours.

Blues and yellows are chosen by people who are content and who have few ambitions.

Dark colours – dark blue and black – are usually chosen by people who are desperate to achieve and usually willing to take risks.

People who prefer greens and browns for carpets, curtains and furniture like to hide away from the world and rest. They are creating a 'nest' for themselves away from the hurly burly of modern life.

The career man who doesn't like risks will choose traditional, patterned wallpaper and will fill his home with family photographs and holiday souvenirs.

You can learn a lot from the name people give to their house. If the house is small but called 'Something House', the owners are desperately trying to give the impression that they are richer than they really are. They want to give themselves an impressive sounding address. If the name is something traditional ('Four Winds', 'Dunroamin', 'The Oaks' etc.), they lack imagination but like security. If the house name is personalised ('Joe's Cabin', 'Dave and Mary'), they have powerful egos. A foreign house name suggests a pretentious approach to life.

Chiming door bells, carriage lamps by the front door, rustic wooden name plates outside the house and gnomes sitting by a pond in the front garden suggest a rather childish sense of humour and an innocent (though unfulfilled) sense of affection for grandeur and luxury.

People who live in a built up area and who keep their double front gates permanently locked may have small children, dogs or no motor car. People who have a car but have no small child or dog and yet keep their drive gates shut are probably exceptionally private individuals – likely to be offended by an intrusion of which there is no prior warning.

Greetings cards

How often do you really look carefully at your birthday and Christmas cards?

If you examine the type of card carefully, you can usually find out quite a lot about the person who sent it.

Birthday cards are usually a more reliable indicator than Christmas cards for the simple but important reason that many people buy their Christmas cards in mixed boxes – the card you get may not have been chosen personally for you. Birthday cards, on the other hand, are much more likely to have been carefully and personally selected.

Here are some tips on how you can 'read' the personalities of the people who have sent you cards.

1. Soppy, romantic card

A soppy card – with or without a soppy, romantic verse – is usually sent by someone who wants more attention from you. The sender is desperate for you to know that he cares a lot about you. He wants to know that the feeling is mutual.

2. Simple, cheap rather unsightly card

Probably chosen and sent in a hurry but someone who doesn't want you to think that you've been forgotten. You're expected to accept the card as a sign that he's had the decency to remember you – you are supposed to feel flattered and delighted (and maybe, slightly grateful).

3. A funny card

A card with a gentle, harmless cartoon on the front is sent

by someone who either knows you very well – and knows that you like that type of card – or by someone who doesn't know you very well at all and has played 'safe'.

4. A dirty card with a rude 'double entendre' message

If sent by a man to a woman is usually a joke – possible sent anonymously – chosen by a man who is embarrassed by sex. If sent by a woman to a man such a card is usually chosen by a sexy woman who isn't shy about making her feelings clear.

5. Card with scenes from nineteenth-century life

Usually chosen by someone who doesn't really like the present. He or she enjoys fantasising about living in the past and probably rejects modern values, modern architecture and so on.

6. A card that contains a photograph of a family group

Usually sent by someone who considers himself to be a 'celebrity' or a 'personality' or, at least, a figure of some importance. Such a card suggests that the sender has a more than healthy ego but is keen to let the recipient know that he is just 'human'. In fact, of course, the card tends to make the sender look even grander and more special than ever – and that is its purpose.

7. Card with an art print on the front

Usually prepared on high quality paper such cards are intended to suggest a sophisticated taste. They are designed to show that the sender is cultured and cultivated.

8. A card with a picture of a product made by sender's company

Pure commerce. Sending the card is a mere advertising stunt taking advantage of the occasion.

9. Enormous, very expensive card – maybe with the sender's name and address printed on it.

Sent by someone who lacks self-confidence and wants to impress you. If the card does not have an address printed on it then it has been bought specially and the sender considers you to be rather special to him. Over-printed cards are sent by people who merely want to impress everyone.

Motor cars

Judging a man by the car he drives can be dangerous and unreliable. Many of the cars on the road are not chosen and bought by individuals – they are company cars, bought in fleets and allocated virtually at random. So making a personality assessment on the basis of the type and colour of car a man drives can be misleading.

But if the type of car is taken together with other factors then the information can be useful. As ever with People Watching, it is important to look at the whole picture before coming to a conclusion.

Here are some of the ways in which you can learn about a man from the car he drives.

Condition of car

If a car is bright, sparkling and gleaming like new – even though it isn't new – then the owner clearly cares a great deal about what other people think of him. The motor car is like an outer skin – it is a clear, outward manifestation of the owner's attitude to life. The regular, weekly cleaning, polishing and waxing is done so that the owner can impress his friends and neighbours as well as strangers. Such an owner is likely to be fastidious, slightly obsessional, neat, punctual and reliable. On the other hand he is also likely to lack ambition, drive or purpose. He rarely works overtime (unless he is paid for it), he has little imagination and knows his rights!

If a car has scratched and dented bodywork, is covered with mud and half filled with sweet wrappers, bits of scrap paper, broken cassette boxes and other bits of waste then the owner is more difficult to classify. He may be simply a slob – whose car reflects his attitude towards life. Or he may be a busy, ambitious, forceful, hard working individual who is simply too busy to waste time cleaning out his motor car. Such a car owner may be a failure or he may be a great success. The one certain conclusion you can draw is that he is not unduly concerned about what other people think of him.

Added extras

Personalised number plates show two things: first, a enormous ego and secondly a tremendous need for public approval and recognition. People who buy personalised number plates are telling the world that they deserve to be recognised, that they want to be looked at and admired and that they are important and successful.

Ornaments – dogs on the back window ledge, small dolls dangling from the driver's mirror etc. – are a sign of homeliness and loneliness. The owner of the car doesn't like being away from home any longer than is necessary and so he tries to make his car as much like home as possible.

A coat hanger in the back of the car (usually with a jacket draped over it) suggests that the driver of the car is neat and fastidious and careful about his appearance. He can't afford to be seen looking scruffy and creased and doesn't want the people he sees to know that he's just spent five hours sitting in a cramped, tiny saloon car. He'd like people to think that he'd travelled in a large limousine or by private helicopter.

The driver almost certainly travels regularly (probably daily) and the rest of his motor car is probably very neat and tidy too.

Stickers attached to the windows announcing that the driver has visited such and such a resort are a sign either that the driver is a family man (and his children wanted the stickers on the windows) or else he is a relatively untravelled person who wants to impress the world.

Tinted windows and huge radio aerials are the cheap equivalents to personalised number plates.

Spoilers fitted to the back of an ordinary saloon car suggest that the driver would really like to be sitting in a sports car. He has a vision of himself as a sporty, free wheeling individual. The spoiler is intended to give the driver's ego a lift and to tell the world that the driver isn't quite as boring as the car might otherwise suggest. (In fact, of course, the driver is probably self centred and boring – a fairly lethal combination).

Colour of car

Red is the most aggressive of all colours. People who choose red motor cars are usually daring, adventurous and assertive. They frequently ignore speed limits and cut up other motorists. People who buy red motor cars are also full of self confidence and a large dose of arrogance. Red cars are involved in more accidents than other colours (partly because red cars irritate other drivers) and get stopped for speeding and other motoring offences more than other drivers (because policemen know that drivers of red cars are more likely to break the speed limit than drivers of other cars).

Other bright colours (yellow, orange etc.) are usually bought by people who have an optimistic nature and are rather cheerful and jolly individuals.

Dark coloured cars (black, dark brown, dark blue etc.) are bought by serious people who tend to take themselves seriously.

Light coloured cars (beige, grey etc.) are driven by people who don't have very strong opinions. These insipid 'non colours' are usually chosen because the owner doesn't want to have to make a statement by choosing a more forceful colour.

Jobs

When trying to judge an individual's personality by the job he does you should remember that there are several ways in which you may be misled:

❋ the job an individual takes may be restricted by the available employment. So, if the only jobs available are working at a large administrative centre then an individual may become an administrator simply because there are no other alternatives, rather than by choice.

❋ family traditions may force an individual into a particular line of work. This can be true as much for professionals (e.g. lawyers, doctors etc.) as for people working in the family business.

❋ luck and chance can play an enormous part in helping an individual select a career. A chance meeting on a train can lead to a new job. An affection for a particular subject at school may have been inspired by a friendship or a 'crush' on a teacher and may then lead a student into a specific line of work.

❋ intelligence or lack of it can have a crucial effect on an individual's work prospects. Someone who is very bright is unlikely to end up working on an assembly line in a car factory. Someone who has hardly got two neurones to rub together is unlikely to become a judge or a brain surgeon (on second thoughts perhaps those are bad examples but I'm sure you get the general idea).

Despite these reservations an individual's job can tell you a lot about his personality.

Almost anything in uniform

A policeman, soldier, sailor, airman, traffic warden, commissionaire, air stewardess etc. but *not* a nurse suggests a need for working as part of a team, a need to share and limit personal responsibility and a desire for clear cut rules by which to work. People who work in uniform tend to have more authority than responsibility and can appear belligerent, obstructive and unimaginative to those who encounter them. This is because they are often belligerent, obstructive and unimaginative individuals. It is interesting to note that some people who do not need to wear uniform choose to do so – for example, school teachers who wear gowns and doctors who insist on wearing white coats when there are no practical reasons for them to do so.

Teaching

School teachers and college and university lecturers are sometimes ravaged by feelings of insecurity and worthlessness. They often find it difficult to cope with the real world where they have to confront their physical and mental equals. They choose, therefore, to spend their working lives with children or young people whom they can impress more easily with their wisdom (and in some cases their physical strength).

Administrators

People who choose to become administrators – whether they work for national government, local government or for big business – tend to be cautious, patient, responsible individuals who do not like taking risks and who prefer security to adventure. Administrators tend to be more interested in index-linked pensions than in profit-related bonuses. Administrators would usually prefer to be paid in cash than in share options. Often obsessional, frequently narrow minded and sometimes bigoted, administrators are usually precise, neat and punctual. They tend to be pessimistic rather than optimistic.

Caring professionals

Under this heading are included doctors, nurses and social workers. Individuals who choose a career in health care or social work usually need to be loved, admired and respected. They are basically loving individuals who are often impractical, inefficient and untidy. They are also often self-centred – they help people because they want to help people and because they get pleasure and satisfaction from it. Arrogance is another common fault among the caring professionals. Because they get used to people relying on them, caring professionals can often become bossy and dictatorial. Incidentally, most of these points are also often true for people working in other 'service' industries as diverse as hairdressing and catering.

Entrepreneurs

Individuals who start and run their own businesses are usually aggressive, assertive and self-confident. If they do not have these qualities then they often fail. The successful entrepreneur will be an optimist and will be extremely ambitious. He will also be imaginative, forceful and creative. Successful entrepreneurs are often very short on self-confidence and fear poverty and failure very strongly – it is this lack of self-confidence and this fear of failure that forces them to work long, hard hours and to put themselves under a great deal of pressure. By working long hours they increase their chances of success. Most entrepreneurs have little patience with administrators or red tape and can, paradoxically, appear to be over full of confidence.

The law

Those who choose to enter the law as a profession tend to be unimaginative and self-confident. They enjoy being in a position of authority and power and are, on the whole, unemotional and thick skinned. They find it easy to be cool and detached when dealing with complex personal problems. They do not easily form opinions and their opinions (when formed) tend to be cautious and conservative. They have few ideals and are largely driven by material urges.

Salesmen

People who 'sell' for a living can, if they are skilled, usually sell anything to anyone. They sell not through a knowledge of a particular subject or because they have the right sort of personality. The good salesman will be cheerful, determined and tenacious. He has a strong, likeable personality and a good memory. He usually likes people and because he likes people other people like him. He is neither shy nor modest. He has enough confidence and self assurance to help keep him going despite failure and adversity. He speaks more than he thinks.

Farmers and gardeners

Most of those who work on the land for a living are independent – the majority are, indeed, 'loners'. They are quiet, shy and not particularly good with other people. They think more than they speak and are often easily offended.

Politicians

Ambitious extroverts. They like being the centre of attention. They like showing off. They are full of self-confidence and lack any sense of embarrassment or self consciousness. They are determined, pugnacious, self assertive and aggressive. They hold strong opinions which they are prepared to change when necessary. Modesty is not a conspicuous fault. Some do care passionately about the world and believe that they have the strength to change things for the better. Others simply care passionately about themselves.

Big company executive

Successful big company executives show an unusual mixture of qualities. They are often ambitious but frequently cautious and careful. They have great aspirations but think carefully before taking risks. They will happily accept payment as stock options or performance related bonuses but they will also insist on large basic salaries and a good mixture of 'perks'. The successful executive will be suspicious, cynical and thoughtful. He need not be imaginative or creative. He will be charming, likeable and quick thinking. He will also be selfish, conceited and arrogant.

Manual workers

Good manual workers are patient, unimaginative and unambitious. They take pride in what they do. They have a modest amount of self-confidence but they are not usually assertive.

Actors, journalists, TV presenters

Superficially they may seem to be full of confidence, to be assertive and to have powerful egos. In fact the confidence is a thin veneer underneath which there are countless layers of self doubt and uncertainty. The 'performer' seems to be assertive and aggressive but is in fact desperate for approval, praise and applause.

Authors

Like to think of themselves as kind, thoughtful, imaginative and sensitive (and wonderful lovers). But, in truth, authors tend to be scruffy, neurotic, paranoid workaholics, riddled with frustrations and constantly close to despair.

Hobbies

You can tell an awful lot about someone from the hobby he chooses. After all, hobbies are carefully and deliberately selected. Few people take up hobbies they don't enjoy or positively dislike.

Gardening

Gentle, patient, peaceful people take up – and enjoy – gardening. People who need to relax – and who can relax – enjoy cultivating flowers and vegetables. Those who are tense and who are unable to relax or slow down don't usually enjoy gardening.

Reading

Those who read a lot are usually imaginative, creative and thoughtful. You can, of course, tell a lot from the type of books that people usually read. Romantic fiction is read by people (usually women) whose lives are rather dull and drab and who obtain their excitement and pleasure from the books they read. Thrillers are read by people who want to escape from the boredom and drudgery of daily life or who want to forget their worries, troubles and anxieties. Biographies and autobiographies are (naturally enough) read by those who are genuinely interested in other people's lives – and who can obtain some satisfaction from the adventures of others. By and large people who like reading biographies are exceptionally curious and even nosey – they are probably not above enjoying a little light local gossip. Educational non fiction – books of self improvement, guide books, advice books etc. – is read by people who are aware of gaps in their knowledge. Science fiction is read by people who tend to be dissatisfied with life and the world as we know it. They escape from their unhappiness and frustrations by 'losing' themselves in unrealistic fiction. The same is true of people who choose to read westerns or historical novels.

Watching TV

People whose major hobby is watching television are rather unimaginative and unambitious. They probably have relatively few genuine or strongly held feelings though they may well have strong opinions about religion and politics. They fill the emptiness in their lives by watching television.

Collecting

Collectors – whether of coins, stamps, beer mats, cigarette cards or pieces of porcelain – are natural hoarders. They are shy, quiet people who enjoy their own company and are usually fairly self-sufficient. They are cautious, systematic, meticulous and slightly obsessional. They dislike change and progress.

Playing games and sports

Those who choose to spend their free time playing games can be divided into two main groups. First, there are the individuals who enjoy solitary sports where confrontations are man to man – such as golf, tennis, skiing etc. Second, there are the individuals who enjoy team games such as football. People who enjoy solitary sports are assertive, self-confident, fairly aggressive. They do not shrink from competition – in fact they rather enjoy it. They are fairly self-sufficient and independent. Individuals who prefer team sports are more sociable. They like being with people, they like sharing responsibility and they probably get as much satisfaction from the companionship that is part of their sport as from the competition.

Watching games and sports

Just as those who play sport can be divided into two groups, the same is true of those who choose to spend their free time watching sports. Individuals who like watching solitary sports (golf, tennis and motor racing) are usually independent souls who like to identify with their favourite heroes. On the other hand people who support teams tend to be gregarious and tend to need to share their enthusiasm. It is no coincidence that few golf or tennis players have fan clubs whereas most football clubs have large and active supporters' clubs.

High risk activities

People who enjoy high risk activities such as climbing, motor racing, skiing, scuba diving etc. usually need the extra excitement and thrills because their daily lives are too tedious and predictable. They enjoy the 'kick' they get from putting their lives at risk. They are more frightened of boredom than they are of death.

Violent sports

Boxing, hunting, shooting (live targets) and fishing are enjoyed by people who are insensitive and unimaginative. Those who enjoy these sports and who get pleasure from killing or hurting their targets are usually of modest intelligence. They are often proud and arrogant and full of self-confidence. It is their lack of imagination and sensitivity which enables these people to obtain pleasure by inflicting pain.

Voluntary work

It is often thought that those who dedicate themselves to voluntary work are inspired by selflessness and generosity. This isn't entirely true. People who spend their free time helping others (this includes serving on committees, fund raising etc.) usually do so partly because they get great satisfaction from what they do. They get a 'kick' out of helping other people, they feel good when they are wanted or needed. Such individuals are often driven by a deep sense of guilt, a feeling of worthlessness and a need to be wanted and admired.

Precision skills

People who like honing their physical skills by practising activities such as clay pigeon shooting, target shooting, archery or carpentry are patient, cautious, deliberate and obsessional. They are usually shy, quiet and self effacing. Such individuals are usually reliable, honest and punctual.

Creative skills

Those who enjoy writing, painting, drawing or sculpting in their spare time (as opposed to professionally) are imaginative and thoughtful. They may find their daily work or daily routine frustrating and unsatisfying. They are quiet, thoughtful and independent.

Investing

Anyone whose hobby involves making money must be ambitious and hungry for success. He will have a streak of ruthless determination and will be driven by a lack of personal confidence and a need for security.

Pets

People don't only often look like the pets they choose – but they often select pets which reflect their personalities. And the more pets of a particular type that someone has then the more that type of pet reflects their personality!

Small dog (quiet)

Rather meek, quiet, self-effacing individual. A rather small personality. Not at all showy. Contemplative and self-sufficient. Thoughtful, probably rather set in her ways (small, quiet dogs are usually owned by women rather than men).

Small dog (noisy)

A busy, effervescent personality. Rather energetic.

Large dog

Ebullient, forceful, aggressive, assertive individual. Determined, powerful personality. Doesn't willingly take 'no' for an answer.

Cat

Cat owners are loving, gentle and reflective. They are independent, rather aloof and cautious. Rather fussy and querulous.

Parrot / cockatoo

A rather unusual, distinctive individual. Maybe slightly eccentric. Rather inquisitive, talkative. Not easily embarrassed.

Tropical fish

Peaceful, relaxed, rather 'laid back'. Gentle and slow. Moves and thinks without haste. Rather timid and apologetic.

Budgie

Bright and busy. Likes to keep involved. Can't rest easily – has to be doing something. Doesn't find relaxation easy.

Habits

The tennis player always bounces the ball five times before serving. The writer spends twenty minutes every morning sharpening his pencils – even though he works at a typewriter. The footballer keeps a special pair of boots for big matches. The motorist always buys his petrol at the same garage. The housewife always does her shopping on the same day of the week. The snooker player can't win a match without his usual cue. The unfaithful husband always clears his throat when he is about to tell a lie.

Habits are rituals which make us feel comfortable but we are often unaware of some of our most established habits.

We often claim that our habits are acquired for practical reasons. But the truth is that they often developed to satisfy our emotional needs. The more habits we have the more nervous, anxious, uncertain, shy and inadequate we are. Our daily habits, our behavioural patterns, are moulded by superstition and anxiety.

The more nervous someone is the more likely he is to have a lot of simple, easily identified habits. You can tell how nervous or edgy someone is by counting the number of simple habits he has. Look through the following list and check out the score. Remember, the more habits someone has the more he is likely to suffer from anxiety.

1. Nervously clears his throat before speaking.

2. Has involuntary tics or twitches.

3. Smokes cigarettes or cigars or a pipe.

4. Regularly sucks at a pen or pencil or at the arm of his spectacles.

5. Has a nervous cough.

6. Repeatedly taps his thumb nail on his teeth.

7. Doodles on any available paper with any available pen or pencil.

8. Persistently taps one or both feet while sitting waiting.

9. Drums his fingers on the table top.

10. Often spends time fiddling with – and straightening out – paper clips.

11. Fiddles incessantly with a pen, watch, brooch, bracelet or some other piece of jewellery.

12. Cannot sit still but has to fidget constantly.

13. Constantly check or combs his hair.

14. Repeatedly buttons and unbuttons his jacket.

15. Sticks his tongue out of the corner of his mouth when he is thinking.

16. Plays frequently with his shirt cuffs, cufflinks or

watch strap.

17. Grinds his teeth while sitting thinking or while sleeping.

18. Blowing nose more than is necessary.

19. Plays with rings on fingers.

20. Sleep walks.

Drinks

You can tell a lot about someone by the drink he chooses when he walks into a bar. Before you make any judgements based on the following information you should make sure that the drink is not being bought to accompany a meal.

Red wine

Down to earth, fun loving, substantial, likes a joke and a laugh. Sociable and easy going.

White wine

Image and fashion conscious. Likes to be seen doing the right things, talking to the right people and drinking the right drink. May drink white wine with a little soda in it.

Sherry

Old fashioned, cautious and reliable.

Beer

Usually drunk by males. Usually the traditional type of male. Regards women with a sexist attitude. Likes to be seen as 'one of the boys'. Would be embarrassed to go into a drinking establishment and order anything other than a beer.

Lager

Young (or young thinking). Rather macho. A little more 'modern' and 'free thinking' than the traditional beer drinker. Doesn't mind women in pubs (the beer drinker doesn't really approve). Rather assertive, modern, ambitious.

Gin

Member of the establishment. Strongly dislikes change. Disapproves of progress on principle. Rather earnest and serious.

Vodka

Likes to be seen to be different. Doesn't like to be one of the herd but in truth is neither an innovative individual nor a free thinker.

Shandy

Cautious, thoughtful and rather shy. Doesn't like the idea of being drunk and out of control and doesn't really like the taste of beer but doesn't like to go into a bar and ask for a non alcoholic drink. Likes a compromise. Tries to avoid difficult situations. Prefers a 'middle of the road' approach.

Whisky *blended*

A serious drinker. Someone who takes his pleasure as seriously as anything else in life.

Whisky *malt*

Careful, choosy, probably rather 'difficult', a perfectionist. Almost certainly intolerant.

Tomato juice

Simple, honest, straightforward and uncomplicated.

Bottled water

Cautious, reluctant to take risks. Pessimistic.

Breasts

Some might scoff at the suggestion that there is any link between the size of a woman's breasts and her personality. And I certainly don't suggest that women who are born with large breasts are born with personalities which are different from those of women with small breasts.

But there is no doubt that the size of her breasts plays such a significant role in a woman's life (and in her emotional development) that it can have a powerful and permanent influence on her personality.

Large breasts

Large breasted women tend to attract more male attention during their formative years. They are often embarrassed by this attention. Consequently, large breasted women often become shy and diffident. They prefer relationships which are not overtly sexual but which are predominantly platonic. Women with large breasts may grow to dislike parties and social events. They may find relationships with the opposite sex difficult to control and may be unreliable employees.

Small breasts

Women with small breasts don't have to put up with male advances (or rude comments) during their formative and difficult teenage years. As a result such women may respond by behaving in a more overtly sexual manner. They often become flirtatious. They may get on better with men than with other women.

Medium breasts

Women whose breasts are well developed but not unduly large usually enjoy more balanced relationships than women with unusually large or exceptionally small breasts.

Beards and moustaches

You can tell quite a lot about a man if he isn't clean shaven. The size and shape of his moustache or beard can tell you a great deal about his personality and approach to life.

Full beard

Men with full, untrimmed (or rarely trimmed) beards are robustly male. They are forceful, dominating and aggressive – not easily oppressed or controlled.

Trimmed beards *all types*

Men with neatly trimmed beards have a strong feminine streak. They are conscious of their appearance and image. They worry a great deal about how others see them. They are eager to be noticed and approved.

Designer stubble

The man who wears a constant face full of shadow may be showing the acceptable face of the late twentieth century macho man (saying, in effect: 'I'm man enough to grow a beard if I want to…'); may be uncertain about his masculinity and sexuality; may be saying to the world that he is deliberately departing from the fashionable androgynous look or may simply be making it clear that he is prepared to be 'different'. It is important not to confuse 'designer stubble' with 'scruff stubble' – the unshaven look worn by the man who is saying:

'I don't have to look smart. I'm important enough to shave when I want to. You take me as you find me.'

Full moustache

Full moustaches are relatively unfashionable these days and are usually worn by men who are either consciously adding strength to a 'weak' face or who are deliberately making themselves noticeable. The man who wears a full moustache usually wants to be noticed, wants to be seen as 'different' and wants to be admired. He is probably conscious of his lack of personality. He has little self-confidence.

Thin moustache

The thin, pencil line moustache is usually worn by a man who is anxious to attract members of the opposite sex. He is probably very careful in the way he dresses and very particular about his clothes and general appearance. He is, in short, a vain man. He is probably full of self-confidence.

Presents

You can tell what people think of you by the gifts they give you – you can guess your public image by the gifts you receive at birthday and at Christmas. It doesn't matter whether the gift comes from a relative, friend, employer or employee! Here are the basic categories of gift…

Personal gifts *non sexual*

If you get socks, gloves, scarves, soap or bath salts then it will be from someone who considers themselves to be close to you in a friendly non sexual sort of way.

Personal gifts *sexual*

Exotic underwear, nightwear and perfume all indicate that the giver either regards your relationship as predominantly sexual or would like your relationship to be sexual.

Useful and practical gifts

Toasters, kettles, electric drills etc. are usually bought by people who think of you in a practical rather than a romantic way. The celebration is merely used as an excuse to buy a new piece of kitchen or household equipment. The giver does not think of you in an intimate way at all.

Hobby or interest gifts

When you receive a well thought out gift which satisfies some personal need or which is designed to help you enjoy a hobby more thoroughly, you can be sure that the giver has made a real effort to find you a gift that will please. The giver cares about you.

And finally...

You can learn a great deal by looking at the clothes that people wear, the luggage they carry, the jewellery they choose and the cars they drive. But you can also learn a lot by looking for the little things – small behavioural patterns, tiny habits, actions and movements that seem irrelevant or incidental but which can be a real giveaway!

Look at the way that people walk, for example.

A man who walks with his back held straight as a ladder and his head held high in the air has probably spent some time in the army. (If he is still in the army or remembers army life fondly then he'll have a classic short back and sides army haircut). A man who walks with a confident rolling gait has probably spent some time as a sailor. And someone who keeps looking around him as he walks is probably frightened of being seen or recognised. He may be on his way to – or from – an illicit appointment.

Watch the way that people use their hands.

A woman who is constantly patting her hair is waiting for someone she wants to please or impress. Look and check what she's wearing to find out who she's waiting for. If she's dressed in a demure suit and carrying a briefcase, it's a business meeting. If she's dressed in something revealing and wearing lots of make up, its a 'date'.

You can learn a lot from watching the way that people distribute their luggage when they get into a train. A woman who stuffs everything onto the overhead rack will probably be happy to talk. A woman who surrounds herself with bags and packages wants to be left alone.

You can even learn a lot from watching the way that people sit down. Think of what happens on a park bench, for example. The woman who wants to be left alone will sit right in the middle of the bench – making it difficult for anyone else to sit down without appearing rude. The woman who isn't desperate to avoid strangers will sit at one end of the bench – making it clear that there is room for someone else. And the woman who is positively inviting companionship will sit two-thirds of the way along the bench – leaving plenty of room for a newcomer who is prepared to sit close to her.

All these are aspects of our behaviour that we can make a conscious effort to change. But there are some giveaway signs that can't be disguised. So, for example, when we become extremely interested in something – or someone – then our pupils get bigger. This response is quite automatic and outside our voluntary control. It's a useful tip to remember. If you're chatting to someone at a party keep your eyes fixed on his. If his pupils enlarge then the chances are that he likes you and is excited by you. (You can even use this information to help you win at cards. If you're playing poker with a stranger and you notice that his pupils suddenly enlarge, the chances are that he's got a good hand.)

PART 2

Some Classical Types

• • • • • • •

• • • • • • • • • • • • • •

WE ARE OF course all different. But there are some easily identifiable 'types' of people that can be classified.

On the pages which follow I have listed some of the well known types of homo sapiens. Learn to recognise some of these 'classic types'. You'll find it amusing, entertaining and instructive. Once you have managed to classify someone you'll be able to predict their movements easily and accurately.

The Social Climber

Loves to be seen in all the right places and with all the right people. He would rather have two days in a grubby boarding house within a hundred yards of the seafront at Cannes than two weeks in a luxury caravan five miles away. He can recognise celebrities at two hundred yards in bright sunshine and loves to eavesdrop on them so that he can toss their *bons mots* into his conversation – 'Bumped into Jack Nicholson in Miami, he was moaning about the crowds and the photographers – said it was worse than ever this year.' Wherever he goes he tries to buy T shirts and sweat shirts that give him an exclusive look. When on holiday he needs a team of friends to carry his stuff down to the beach. He has a boat (usually an inflatable dinghy with a huge outboard motor) and the first thing he does on the beach is put up a canvas windscreen and a huge sun shade with CINZANO on it. He has an underwater camera and instead of playing badminton with cheap plastic rackets insists on playing French boules with steel balls carried in smart leather pouches. He has a small portable TV and always chooses food that no one (including him) can pronounce. At home he lives in a small, suburban villa with two and a half bedrooms and a sixteenth of an acre of garden. He has little self-confidence and desperately wants other people to see him as a success.

The Wimp

Always apologetic and diffident. Nervous and never lets his emotions show in public. Subscribes to the *Readers Digest* and quotes the articles he reads at great length. Rarely has any original ideas or opinions of his own. He always carries a briefcase with him wherever he is going. Inside it usually contains a few copies of his trade journal, a three year old congratulatory memo from the Chairman's Executive Assistant and a banana. He always wears black lace up shoes or brown sandals. His socks are invariably grey. He is so thin that when he undresses you could tap out a reliable beat on his ribs. Wherever he goes he spends most of his time in queues. He queues for ice cream, cups of tea and lavatories. He is very pale and never takes part in games of any sort. He wears spectacles (always carries a spare pair in case of emergencies) and has several pens clipped into the outside breast pocket of his rather cheap and worn jacket. His trousers are shiny at the knees and where he sits down. If he's on the beach he sits on the rocks at the back. If he goes swimming he leaves his sandals at the water's edge with his socks stuffed inside them. He always carries an umbrella or a plastic mac – sometimes both. He is harmless but contributes little to life. His main aim is to get through life without any confrontations. Is likely to have a nervous breakdown if faced by a major crisis (e.g. late arrival of *Readers Digest*).

The Misery

Is always moaning. At work he complains about the boss, the trade union, the suppliers and the central heating. In the pub he complains about the price of beer, the state of the nation and the décor. On holiday he complains that it's too windy or too hot. He reaches a peak of unhappiness abroad where he suddenly loves his country and hates all foreigners. (There is too much sand everywhere. The sun is too hot. There are too many flies. It is too far to the toilets and the toilets are always disgusting. The ice creams are too expensive. The sea smells funny. The beach is too crowded. The place is too noisy. There is tar and sewage all over the place. The children are too noisy. The naked bodies are shocking. The newspaper is too late arriving. The food is terrible. The beer is weak and watery. The roads are too crowded. The airport is smelly and overcrowded. The natives are rude and they steal.) He is a complete pessimist. He never goes anywhere without his folding umbrella. When eating an ice cream he wraps a tissue around his hand and puts a hanky on his knee. After he's eaten it he becomes convinced that he's about to die of food poisoning. He enjoys being miserable and rarely gets enthusiastic about anything.

Power Woman

Has a male assistant who is ten years older than her and who dresses impeccably and wears an old Etonian tie. Has a male secretary and a male chauffeur – both of whom are tall, handsome and perfectly groomed. She wears simple but expensive business suits – all made by Chanel – and carries a thin alligator skin briefcase with her at all times. Her assistant carries the portable telephone. She is attended twice a week in her office by a beautician and every morning at 7.00 by her hair-dresser. She plays tennis on Mondays, Wednesdays and Fridays at a private club and swims on Tuesdays and Thursdays. When invited to dinners and other public occasions she uses an escort provided by a discreet male escort agency. It is made quite clear to the escort that he is not regarded as anything other than an essential accessory – a stage prop. Her sex life (if she has one) is a mystery to everyone with whom she does business although it is rumoured that she has a cottage in the country to which she retires, apparently alone, for long weekends. She has a fine figure and shapely legs which she is not above displaying if meetings do not seem to be going her way. She often appears essentially masculine in her outlook but is, in fact, 100% female. She uses her masculine veneer to stun her competitors and her feminine wiles to distract them while contracts are being drawn up.

Power Man

Never has breakfast alone or with his family. Breakfasts are for business meetings in large, five star hotels. He drinks vast quantities of orange juice and nibbles unconvincingly at a croissant. Before breakfast spends half an hour in the gym or at his club's private swimming pool. Has a sophisticated computer operated exercise bicycle in his study at home and a skiing machine in his office. He has a private shower suite attached to his office so that he can shower and refresh himself after his regular bouts of exercise. Dresses to impress not to keep warm or feel comfortable. Has suits which are made for him by an expensive tailor, shoes which are individually hand crafted by a skilled boot maker and shirts which are hand made in white silk and monogrammed on the pockets. Travels in a large BMW or Mercedes which is fitted with two telephones, a fax machine and a small computer. Never goes anywhere without a smartly dressed male assistant. Has one secretary (a stunningly beautiful 26-year-old blonde) to impress visitors and another (an efficient but rather dowdy 55 year old) to do the work. His chauffeur wears a cap and uniform. Never carries a briefcase (his assistant carries it for him) or an umbrella or overcoat (it's twelve years since he last walked anywhere or stepped out of his car onto anything other than a red carpet). Has cultivated a firm, penetrating stare and uses a thin, gold Cartier pen to make notes on a tiny leather bound notepad. Always seems strong, powerful and in control. In fact he is terrified of failure and poverty and works 18 hours a day. If deprived of the trappings of power and success he would not survive for five minutes.

The Empty Suit

He always wears a suit — usually a cheap one bought ready-to-wear from a chain of men's outfitters. He has no original ideas and no personal opinions. Whoever hires his body also hires his mind (such as it is) in its entirety. He does not usually work alone but prefers to operate as a member of a group. He is always careful to agree with everything the leader of his group might say. He never voices any criticism of the group or the 'management'. He can, however, be ruthless and cruel when dealing with those who have more responsibility than authority. He dislikes creative individuals or thinkers whom he distrusts and fears. He worries more about his own status and position within the company than about the company's long-term future. He works from 9 to 5 — arriving strictly on time and leaving precisely at 5. The only thing he really cares passionately about are his pension arrangements. He is narrow minded, bigoted and unimaginative. He has few personal ambitions (other than to survive within the system and to rise to a higher position within the establishment of which he is a firmly committed member). Although aggressive to those who he considers to be his social inferiors, he is obsequious and fawning to those who he regards as his superiors.

The Pseudo Intellectual

Male version always wears cord trousers or jeans and old jacket – preferably with leather patches on the elbows. Female version wears black, dark blue or purple and prefers to wear clothes made out of the sort of material they used to use when making table cloths. Is desperately interested in Samoan poetry. Smokes small quantities of marijuana on Saturday evenings. Takes selenium and manganese supplements every day. Has written an article on the plight of hill farmers in Argentina. Writes bad poetry and has had several poems printed in a small, privately published poetry magazine. Only ever watches films in French or Italian (preferably in original version without subtitles). Doesn't watch much television but prefers documentary programmes about shipbuilding in Korea and desert irrigation in North Africa. Once provided technical advice for a television programme about rivet making in Chicago in the 1930s. When eating out always chooses ethnic restaurants – preferably serving an obscure type of Indonesian food. Drives a very small, ecologically sound French car (a Citroen, Renault or Peugeot). Smokes Gauloise cigarettes incessantly. Lectures twice a week on seventeenth-century English poetry at the local college – to a class that never contains more than four pupils. Trained as a school teacher or social worker but currently holds well paid position with fund raising group. Would desperately like to be a real intellectual but has neither the brains nor the academic knowledge so disguises these shortcomings by concentrating all his or her efforts on minority subjects.

The Hypochondriac

Talks incessantly about his or her health. Invariably has several pill bottles in handbag or jacket pocket and frequently has a recent operation to discuss. Meal times are a nightmare for hostesses. Can't eat red meat, green vegetables or brown bread. Can't eat anything with roughage in it. Can't eat anything that contains fat. Has an allergy to most common fruits and develops a severe attack of wheezing if anyone at the same table so much as looks at a tomato or strawberry. Has to eat food that is entirely free of salt because of family blood pressure problems. Doesn't like being in the sunlight because of the risk of skin cancer. Doesn't like open fires or lit candles because of the toxic hydrocarbons. Has weak knees and a weak back. Carries a packet of antiseptic wipes to clean cutlery and crockery when eating out (just in case the waiter has any nasty diseases). Won't sleep on a bed that doesn't have at least one door stuffed underneath the mattress. Can't wear clothes made out of nylon or any other man made fibre. Animal furs produce skin reactions. Suffers from chest pains which come on if exposed to excitement or any threat. Has a bladder problem so doesn't like to travel far from a lavatory. In any group of people is very probably the fittest person there. Genuinely enjoys ill health. Originally used illness to make himself/herself interesting. Is now totally obsessed by the imagined malfunctioning of his or her body.

The Beautiful Person

Has dedicated his or her life to the worship of high fashion. Deeply suntanned, drenched with expensive perfume or aftershave. Invariably overdressed whatever the occasion. Talks incessantly about St Moritz and Bermuda. Wears clothes by Yves St Laurent or Ted Lapidus. When sunbathing uses a metal reflector to ensure that the area underneath his or her chin is evenly tanned. Uses small cardboard toe dividers to make sure that the sun can get to the little areas between the toes. Removes any excess or unwanted hair the moment it appears. Won't wear anything with a stain on it or a crease in it. Uses designer luggage with the designer's name clearly visible. Goes skiing every year and always has a new skiing outfit. Practises quietly and privately on a dry ski slope so that he/she can appear confident and skilled on the slopes. Only ever drinks French wine. In fact probably has a really dull life. May have inherited money from rich aunt. May have a monthly allowance from parents. Or may work as Regional Sales Manager for large organisation. Latter is most likely. Sustains sun tan by regular use of sun bed at works swimming pool complex.

The Thrill Seeker

Some people love danger. They live for it. They need it and thrive on it. The 'thrill seeker' is a daredevil. He may become a criminal, a delinquent, a war hero, a champion skier, a racing car driver, or a creative or performing genius. He will probably be loved dearly and expansively by many people. But he will be hated by others. He will on occasions show astonishing levels of brilliance. But he will also be unreliable, unpredictable and uncontrollable. He will be difficult, rude and aggressive. He will show contempt for authority and will pursue the unknown and the uncertain with constant affection. To him danger is a friend not a threat. He will have an enormous amount of natural talent. He will get tremendous satisfaction when his talents work well. But he will also suffer deep despair and depression when things go wrong. He will not cope well with drudgery and routine work. He will be easily bored. He is not frightened by death. In fact, on the contrary, he regards death as a challenge, a competitor to be taken on and beaten. He works best in a crisis, when the odds are against him. He finds routine work uninteresting and uninspiring. He is, surprisingly, relatively unambitious. He is driven not by material success or by rewards or praise or by achievements but by thrill and excitement. He may be inspired by the roar of the crowd but the approval of the establishment means little to him.

The Workaholic

He cannot ever rest. He drives himself all the time. However much money he makes, however successful he becomes he has to continue to push himself. He arrives early at work and leaves late at night. He takes little time for lunch. He takes work home with him in the evenings and at weekends. He rarely, if ever, takes a holiday. If he does go away for a few days he frets and worries. He only feels comfortable if he can telephone his office and check that all is well. His briefcase is full of papers which he needs to read. His desk is never clear of paperwork. He has two in trays and two out trays and drives his secretary hard. He pushes himself because when he was small his parents never praised him or told him that they loved him. They took his achievements for granted. He always wanted to be told that they were proud of him. He wanted to be told that they loved him. But they were cool and detached and so he tried harder and harder. Now, as an adult, he is still trying to gain the love and approval that he never had as a child. He pushes himself constantly. He probably suffers from indigestion, headaches, chest pains and other stress induced diseases.

The Money Minded

His sole purpose in being alive is to make money – and to make sure that everyone around knows how much money he has got. He is completely selfish and is dedicated to earning money and acquiring new possessions. He spends some time and effort exercising and eating the right sort of foods but only so that he can maintain his health so that he can work harder and more effectively and earn more money. When buying a house or flat he thinks of it as an investment rather than a home. He buys a run-down house in a smart area and then proceeds to tear out the guts, paint everything white and fill it with expensive furniture (bought partly for its investment qualities and partly to make the house look attractive to a prospective buyer). You can easily recognise the house he lives in – there is always a skip outside that is filled with cracking linoleum and old fashioned bedroom suites. He jogs every morning (part of his attempt to get fit for business) and wears a smart, coloured jogging suit and a pair of expensive jogging shoes. At Christmas he buys his friends ski wax or computer programs as presents. He never eats junk food. He doesn't have much time for sex – regarding it as a rather futile, unnecessary and entirely unprofitable waste of time for anyone who doesn't do it professionally. He does not believe in sharing his wealth with anyone. He is firmly dedicated to the theory that the meek are not entitled to expect anything. His values are strictly conservative.

Medallion Man

It can be a small gold ingot, a St Christopher, an Egyptian sex sign or an initial (his own of course). It can be made of gold or silver. It hangs around his neck and nestles in a thick matting of tightly curled black hair which glistens with drops of expensive sun tan oil. He dresses impeccably with his shirt open to the waist (so that the medallion from which he gets his name can be seen) and his slacks neatly pressed. He drives a secondhand Porsche or a Ford with all the available trimmings. When going out to dinner he wears a blue blazer with gold buttons on it. His hair is always neatly trimmed and never out of place. He spends most of his free time just walking about – he doesn't like to sit down in case he creases or dirties his trousers. He tries to pay for everything (even items costing only a few pence) with his American Express gold credit card so that as many people as possible can see that he has got one. He is narcissistic, selfish and self-confident. He has little time for anyone else. Whenever a conversation starts he always expects it to be about him – if it isn't then he soon makes sure that it is.

The Plastic Box Lady

Wherever she goes she takes an entire kitchen full of equipment with her. If going for a picnic in the country she has to start planning at least three days beforehand. If going down onto the beach she gets her husband to get up early and mark off her patch in a suitable position just on the safe side of the high tide mark. She needs quite a large area for all her equipment. The centre point of her activities is a large plastic table cloth held down by four huge stones. She has matching plastic crockery and cutlery and an apparently endless number of sealed plastic boxes. She is, for example, certain to keep the tomatoes in a separate container from the lettuce. The picnic hamper and cool boxes that she uses seem to defy all laws of size and space. At all picnics she will produce such essentials as a bottle of salad cream, a bottle of tomato ketchup and two varieties of brown sauce. She spends all her life preparing meals. She is remarkably capable in emergencies and it is difficult to think of a crisis for which she would not be prepared. If a volcano suddenly erupted underneath her she would probably be handing out anti volcano tablets and burn cream within thirty seconds.

The Hunk

The hunk works out in the gym for most of the year. His two week beach holiday is the highlight of his year. It gives him a chance to show off his body. He comes down to the beach in cut down jeans and a pure white singlet that shows off his tanned muscles perfectly. He plays beach games constantly and always hits the ball miles into the air. He loves to get into arm wrestling contests – preferably with lots of people watching. His favourite trick is to persuade a friend to bet him that he can't do 100 press ups with a girl sitting on his shoulders. He always manages it with ease, of course. If he goes swimming he wears the briefest of swimming trunks. His favourite game is volleyball. Can often be seen strutting around with a surfboard under his arm. He is probably the only human being in the whole world who eats ice cream by biting it. He is not endowed with too large a brain. His body is largely muscle and his head is largely bone.

The Tease

At the disco she wears a very short skirt, stockings and suspenders. Plus a low cut top. She bends forwards and backwards a lot so that the boys and young men around get a good look at her thighs and breasts. If she wears a bra it is designed to draw attention to her breasts. On the beach she wears the tiniest of bikinis and unties the straps of her bikini top to ensure an even all-over tan (even though the straps aren't more than a few fractions of an inch wide). She constantly finds excuses for sitting up suddenly – but is extremely adept at catching hold of herself before anything essential is revealed. She is likely to encourage casual acquaintances to put sun oil on her back and legs. When playing beach games jumps up and down a lot so that her breasts bounce around and attract a lot of attention. Takes ages getting dressed under cover of a towel that is just large enough but small enough not to look large enough. In the sea she always squeals a lot and pretends to have almost lost her bikini top. When eating an ice cream she licks it slowly – but only when she's made sure that at least one member of the opposite sex is watching her. If approached by a male will usually giggle and run off with her girlfriend. However old she is, her emotional age is about fifteen.

The Flirt

An older version of 'The Tease'. Usually in her forties. She flirts outrageously with everyone else's husband, lover, boyfriend, father or brother. She insists on being kissed on the cheek by every male she meets who is over the age of sixteen. Links arms with any half way presentable male and hugs him to her possessively. She wears rather too much make up and clothes that are either just a little too tight or else just a touch too revealing. She is usually married but her marriage is not a happy one. Her husband is away from home a lot of the time. She is desperately lonely and wants to be loved and wanted. The odd thing is despite her behaviour she is unlikely to have ever received a serious response from any of the men she has flirted with. It is difficult to guess how she would respond if she did receive an immodest proposal. The chances are that she would be startled, shocked, dismayed and slightly disgusted and would hurry away and cry herself to sleep.

The Lion

He is a natural leader. He is courageous, assertive, powerful and responsible. He takes responsibility naturally and with ease. He is confidently at ease when under pressure. He has sound principles and attracts a considerable amount of loyalty from those who work with him. He is generous, kind and thoughtful. He never takes advantage of people who work with him. When things go well for him he shares his good fortune with those who are close to him. He is honest and reliable and would be hurt, offended and upset if he thought that anyone thought him otherwise. He does not believe in sharing his emotions with anyone. If someone offends him in some way he will say nothing but nurse his grievance close to his heart. He would be deeply ashamed and embarrassed if a tear escaped from an eye and he would rather die than bang his fist or shout at anyone. He can show violent anger and distress with a raised eyebrow and a lift of his head. He is honourable and proud. He is quite likely to be taken advantage of by people who are less confined by a sense of right and wrong.

The Fox

He is cunning, sly and quick witted. He has a strong sense of self preservation. He is very much an individual rather than a member of a group. He is a master of the compromise and is a skilful, experienced and wary negotiator. He never fits easily into any group and his loyalty is always to himself. He almost certainly works for himself (rather than a company). He may be in the 'import-export' business or he may be an agent or representative. He is a wheeler dealer and loves the thrill of a good, drawn out, carefully structured negotiation. He is patient, careful and cautious and is prepared to plan carefully for the future. He can be arrogant and conceited but can also be extraordinarily charming. If he thinks that there is something to be gained in the long term he can be generous and kindly in the short term. He will happily invest the price of a good meal for a prospect of a possible, profitable future deal. He has few genuine friends – most of the people he knows are business contacts. He would never put a mere friendship above a profitable deal.

The Health Freak

Unlike the hypochondriac, who is always moaning about some illness or other, the health freak is always boasting about how healthy she is. She spends an enormous amount of time and money trying hard to maintain her health. She buys (and dutifully swallows) a host of vitamin and mineral supplements every day. She is an enthusiastic vegetarian and she has a collection of cookery books designed to help make dinner parties and barbecues exciting. She is proud of her body and even prouder of the fact that she hasn't had a cold for eleven years. She claims that this is because of the vitamins she swallows. She has an ioniser in the bedroom and another one in her office. She is contemplating buying a radiation shield to put into the loft. She only ever drinks bottled water. She avoids foods that contain additives. She subscribes to a health newsletter and never accepts medical opinion without asking for additional advice. She regularly visits an osteopath and naturopath and spends at least one week a year at a health farm where she can rest and relax. She meditates every morning and every evening for thirty seconds. For her good health is an end in itself. She has no other great interests in her life.

The Androgynous Male

He is very sensitive to women's rights. He gets easily offended when he thinks he has spotted another sign of women being oppressed. When he takes a woman out for a meal he insists on sharing the cost with her so as not to offend her. He would not dream of standing up on a bus to offer a woman a seat because he would regard that as a sexually aggressive and patronising thing to do. He cries easily and readily when he is upset and believes that all men should let their emotions show. When making love to a woman he is always sensitive to her needs and he is generally regarded as a kind, patient and tolerant friend. He proudly claims that he always understands the needs of others and he says that he sympathises with all oppressed minorities. He strongly believes that most men still treat women without sufficient respect.

The Androgynous Female

She is aggressive, assertive and dominating. She believes that since men have for centuries taken advantage of women it is up to women to redress the balance. She has little love for or sympathy with men. She dresses in dark, shapeless clothes because she believes that pretty clothes are merely designed to titillate that male appetite. She has not worn a bra for 17 years and regards stockings and suspenders as obscene and pornographic items of clothing. She is argumentative and constantly ready to argue that women have made major but unheralded contributions to science and the arts. She believes that a world without men would be pleasant and (thanks to the existence of modern technology) entirely possible. She has no sense of humour and regards comedians, comics and books of humour as generally irrelevant.

The Trend Follower

Difficult to describe. By the time you read this whatever is fashionable as I write will be laughably out of date. The 'trend follower' was the first person on his block to wear a digital watch or to discover two tone shoes and the first to abandon both when they went out of fashion again. He is wearing trousers with turn ups the third time round while others are still wearing them on the first time round! His major anxiety is of appearing out of date. He is a regular reader of fashion magazines. His own personal tastes have long since been lost and forgotten. His taste in music, food, drink and architecture is similarly inspired by fashion.

PART 3

How to
Manipulate People

· ·

● ● ● ● ● ● ● ● ● ● ● ● ● ● ●

Learning how to 'read' people is fun. But once you've learned how to understand why people behave the way they do you can use your knowledge to help you in many different ways.

In this, the third and final part of the book, I have outlined some of the ways in which you can use your People Watching skills to your advantage.

How to look sexy *for men*

🧍 Stand with your shoulders held back to make yourself look as tall and as broad as possible. If you have the beginnings of a paunch try to hold it in (better still, try to lose it).

🧍 Walk 'tall' – making the most of your height. Stick out your chest and walk with a bit of a swagger. The non sexy man walks with a stoop and looks as though he has the worries of the world on his shoulders. His walk shows that he lacks determination, aggression or any sense of excitement. (Although, of course, if you manage to look unhappy enough and unfortunate enough there is always a chance that you'll find a woman prepared to 'mother' you into bed.)

🧍 Never have pens in your breast pocket (they suggest that you have a modest, clerical job). Nor should you have a neatly folded handkerchief in that pocket (that suggests that you are very conventional and rather obsessional – hardly an exciting prospect as a lover).

🧍 Stand with your thumbs tucked into your belt or with your hands on your hips (*both* hands, not one hand on one hip). This will make you look fairly aggressive and masculine. Push your crotch forwards slightly – but don't overdo it or you'll look rather comical.

♟ Wear a signet ring if you like but not a wedding ring. A signet ring shows loyalty. Men usually wear wedding rings because their wives want them to wear them.

♟ If you wear a tie choose something plain and keep the knot loose. If you don't wear a tie then leave the top two buttons of your shirt unfastened to give just a hint of what is there. Don't have your shirt unbuttoned to the waist and don't have a medallion of any kind hanging around your neck. Remember that toothpaste on your shirt and egg on your tie are unlikely to send a woman into a frenzy of excitement.

♟ Hold up your trousers with a very thin belt. A large belt suggests that you are worried about losing your trousers. Avoid braces for the same reason. And never, never wear a belt and braces – that suggests that you are a cautious pessimist (and very boring).

♟ Be clean shaven. Beards are out. Sideburns are out. Moustaches are very difficult to get right. Designer stubble is out of fashion unless you match it with the scruffy 'rough' look.

♟ The first thing a woman looks at will probably be your hair. So take care of it. A loose style is better than anything tight or too formal.

♟ Avoid silly shoes (e.g. cowboy boots). Choose either well polished shoes or smart, new trainers.

♟ Below the belt wear either skimpy briefs, brightly coloured or patterned boxer shorts or lacy French knickers. Muddy coloured Y fronts are out. Socks should be short and brightly coloured. Do not wear long socks held up with suspenders. Avoid dull coloured underwear. Avoid string vests at all costs. Men's underwear always looks silly. Don't make things worse than they need be.

♠ Stand with your body facing the woman you fancy – with at least one foot pointing directly at her.

♠ Sit with your legs wide apart or at least one knee pointing at the woman you're interested in.

♠ If a woman is looking straight at you check your tie and your hair. The 'preening' moves are a sign of courtship that are recognised by a woman's unconscious mind.

♠ When speaking lower the pitch of your voice as much as you comfortably can to make yourself more macho.

♠ Drink lager from a straight sided glass – in pints not halves. Never touch anything with ice in it. Never drink funny coloured concoctions that come with lots of umbrellas.

♠ Drive something with character. Not necessarily a sports car, not necessarily expensive. Four wheel drive covered in mud is sexy. Body damage is sexy. Do not drive anything with stickers on the windows, nodding dogs on the back shelf or deodorisers and stick-on compasses on the dashboard.

♠ Send flowers and simple greetings cards to show that you care. Never send 'sexy' or rude greetings cards.

♠ Look the woman you fancy straight in the eye – to make sure that you've got her attention.

♠ Never stand with your arms crossed in front of your chest or with your hands clasped in front of your crotch. Both positions suggest that you are extremely defensive.

How to look sexy for women

🧍 Stand with your shoulders pushed back to exaggerate the size and shape of your breasts. If you stand hunched then your breasts will sag and (if they are small) almost disappear.

🧍 Always carry a small handbag to give an impression of helplessness. Don't carry a huge, capacious handbag that looks as if it contains a full set of car tools, a diesel generator in case there is a power cut and a spare gallon of petrol. A large handbag will give the impression that you are totally independent and do not need to be protected by a male. Men like to feel that they are needed.

🧍 Stand with your legs slightly apart, with one knee or foot pointing towards the man you fancy. This subtle body language will attract his attention. Do not keep your legs pressed tightly together.

🧍 Do wear a necklace of some kind to draw attention to your breasts. If you wear a brooch make sure that it is pinned in such a place that it will draw attention to your bosom.

🧍 Touch your hair frequently to attract attention to yourself. Do not wear your hair in a tight bun – that looks efficient rather than erotic.

🧍 Keep your arms away from your body. Folding your arms across your chest hides your charms and makes you look defensive. If you want to look really sexy tuck one thumb into your belt or rest your hand upon one hip to display confidence and show a little aggression.

🧍 Don't wear low heeled shoes that do nothing for the shape of your legs. Instead wear high heeled shoes that tighten up the muscles in your legs and make them look shapely. Most men find high heeled shoes erotic.

♟ Do not speak too loudly or confidently if you do not want to frighten prospective suitors away. (But don't whisper in a 'bedroom' voice or speak in a low 'little girl lost' voice.)

♟ Usually the first thing a man looks at when he meets a woman is her eyes. So take care with your eye make up – and check it frequently. If you see a man you fancy look straight into his eyes to show that you find him attractive – glancing upwards or sideways occasionally to show that you are shy.

♟ When sitting make sure that you show an inch or two of knee – just as a taste or touch of temptation.

♟ Lick your lips frequently to make them moist. Use lipstick to keep them red. Keep your lips slightly apart in a blatantly sexual gesture.

♟ Touch yourself frequently – on your thighs for example.

♟ Fondle anything sexually symbolic that comes your way – a wine glass stem, a cigarette lighter, a pen or pencil or a cigarette. If you have a drink in a pub choose wine – that comes in a delicate, 'feminine' glass with a stem that you can fondle – rather than beer that comes in a mug and makes you look like one of the boys.

♟ Chose clothes that are tight and figure hugging (to show off your figure) or loose and billowy (to hide your figure and increase the mystery).

♟ Choose underwear with him in mind – lacy half cup bra; skimpy lacy knickers; stockings and suspenders. If you're really feeling racy then your stockings will be seamed. If you are a sex bomb wear no underwear at all – apart from three dabs of perfume. Don't wear warm, sensible underwear (coloured grey) that you've bought in the sales; and never wear highly coloured tights.

♟ When you walk roll your hips, deliberately and provocatively pushing your bottom from side to side. The non sexy woman moves with a flat footed determined gait that leaves everything to the imagination.

♟ Wear ear rings and finger rings to draw attention to yourself and make yourself look feminine. The non sexy woman wears no jewellery apart from badges which carry political slogans.

♟ If you have a motor car choose something small, sexy and feminine. Don't drive around in anything too large, powerful and aggressive.

♟ If you send a greeting card choose something full of saucy drawings and double meanings in order to show that you're broad minded and full of fun.

♟ Choose brightly coloured clothes whenever you can. The non sexy woman chooses clothes that are designed purely and simply to keep her dry, warm and decent.

How to look like a winner

The secret of looking like a winner is simple – you must look the way that other people expect a winner to look!

Here are the rules!

☑ First and foremost you must decide whom you want to impress. Who do you want to think of you as a winner? Unless you know your 'market' then you can't prepare your image properly. If you want to make the manager at the bank think of you as successful then you'll probably have to buy and wear a suit. But if you want to look like a successful rock star then a suit is hardly likely to help your public image.

☑ Whatever clothes you wear your teeth and nails should

be well looked after. Your teeth should be white and, if necessary, capped. Your nails should be clean and cut short. And unless you are already so successful that people know that you are a winner you should take care with your hair.

☑ Your clothes should be well fitting, well made and made out of good material. The cut is more important than the age. If you can only afford one inexpensive suit, buy a good, secondhand one that fits rather than a cheap one off the peg.

☑ If you wear spectacles, take great care with the frames. If you only have one pair, make sure that you buy frames that are classic not fashionable. Look at some photographs of people who look like winners – see what sort of spectacle frames they are wearing. Don't buy unusual or fashionable frames unless you have plenty of money and can afford to buy several pairs.

☑ Write with an expensive pen – preferably a fountain pen rather than a ballpoint pen. Ideally you should have a fountain pen that needs filling up from a bottle of ink. Black ink is best. Brown ink will do if you want to look rather eccentric. Blue ink is rather common. Any other colour is just too eccentric.

☑ If you carry a briefcase, if it is new it should be thin and have gold locks but no initials. If it is old it can be whatever shape you like but should be battered and well worn. Large, black, plastic briefcases suggest that you have to carry around samples and sales literature. Winners do not carry such briefcases.

☑ When you meet people look them in the eye – to dominate them right from the start. Losers hold their eyes down, look away or look at the floor.

☑ If you have a thin or weedy voice spend some time training yourself to speak in a more aggressive and forceful manner. No one takes a thin or weedy voice seriously – and if you don't sound like a winner then you'll never be treated like one. These days a good telephone voice is essential – and if you're going to be a winner you're going to have to appear on television and radio and you're going to have to give public speeches.

☑ If you work in an office in a large company establish some mild but luxurious eccentricities.

☑ If you have pictures up on your office walls they should be pictures of famous and influential people – preferably signed with best wishes to you. You don't actually have to get such pictures signed. It will do if you can get hold of ordinary photographs and then scribble a message on yourself. It's not who you know that counts – but who other people *think* you know.

☑ If everyone else in your company has one phone on their desk make sure that you get two phones. And try to make sure that your phones are a different colour to everyone else's. Try also to make sure that you have a special type of phone – with lots of 'hold' buttons.

☑ If you want to impress people, get yourself paged at all the best places. When you know that your boss is at a sporting event, have your name called out over the loud speaker system. When you know that your boss is visiting the opera, have yourself discreetly paged. When your boss is having tea at a hotel have a bellhop wander about with your name on a small blackboard. Slowly, but surely, your image and reputation will be enhanced. You will begin to sound like a winner and people will think of you as a winner. Once people think of you as a winner then you will be a winner.

☑ Money spent on obviously expensive luxuries is money well spent. When you're applying for a job hire a really expensive car for the day. Hire an expensive suit. Borrow a really expensive watch. Have your CV professionally printed. If you have faith in yourself then you must invest in yourself.

How to tell if someone is bored

How can you tell if someone is bored with you? How can you tell if your speech is boring the pants off the assembled listeners?

🐢 People who are bored will frequently cross and uncross their legs.

🐢 Another sign of boredom is to allow one leg to move up and down, keeping the ball of the foot on the ground while tapping the heel rhythmically.

🐢 Yawning is a sign of boredom.

🐢 Look at the eyes. The eyes of a bored individual will flicker from side to side in search of greater stimulation.

🐢 Someone who is bored by what you are saying will find it difficult to pay attention. He will, therefore, have to ask you to repeat what you have said.

🐢 The ultimate sign of boredom is a snore – a sign that you have sent your audience off to sleep.

How to tell if someone is left handed

How many people do you know who are left handed?

It's a simple question but you're probably never even

thought about it before.

And yet the information can sometimes be vitally important.

Of course, the simplest way to find out if someone is left handed is to watch which hand they use when they write. Ninety per cent of the population are right handed and so individuals who are left handed tend to stand out.

Here, however, are some simple tricks that you can use to help you tell whether someone you know is left or right handed.

Most people wear their watch on their 'weak' side. In other words someone who is right handed will wear his watch on his left wrist while someone who is left handed will wear his watch on the right hand.

Right handed people usually part their hair on their left side. And left handed individuals usually part their hair on their right side.

People who wear a belt to hold up their trousers wear it so that the tip of the belt points to their weak side. So, a man who is right handed will wear his belt in such a way that the loose tip of it points to the left.

If an individual has two pockets in his jacket or shirt then he will usually carry personal items (wallet, sunglasses, cigarettes etc.) in the pocket that is on his weak side. So, a man who is left handed will have his sunglasses in the pocket on his right side.

A right handed man who carries his wallet in the back pocket of his trousers will usually carry it in the right hand pocket (this information is only useful if he has a choice of two pockets). The left handed individual will, of course, carry his wallet in the left hand pocket.

👆 Most individuals hold the shoulder on their strong side slightly lower than the shoulder on their weak side.

How to understand other people

If you understand how other people think then you can predict what they will do and you can plan and control your life much more efficiently and effectively. Understanding other people is the most basic and fundamental part of knowing how to manipulate people and get them to do what you want them to do and to behave in the way you would like them to behave!

In order to understand how people think you must know their secret fears, desires, guilts and aspirations. Remember everyone has fears, desires, guilts and aspirations – even the hardest and toughest businessman is besieged by them.

If you know someone's fears then you know his weaknesses and inadequacies and you can use those weaknesses either to help you stop him worrying (and feel more comfortable) or to help you make him feel on edge and uncomfortable.

The secret of understanding other people, therefore, is to know what they worry about.

Here is a list of the things that people worry about. These simple categories cover just about everything anyone is likely to fear. When you meet someone for the first time – and it is important that you understand him well – then ask yourself into which of these categories his personal fears are most likely to fall.

Health

Top of any normal person's list of worries is health. People worry about their health because they don't like the idea of being ill, in pain and incapable and they (mostly) hate the idea of dying. It is because of this natural fear of illness that doctors have such a strong hold over most of their patients. Very few people will argue with a doctor or complain about him to his face – their fear of illness is easily translated into respect for his knowledge and power. (In a later section I will describe how you can manipulate your doctor subtly and easily.) The big, red faced, aggressive businessman may seem not to care about his health as he downs another double whisky and puffs at his huge cigar but he does care. He worries about his blood pressure. He worries about heart disease. He worries about lying in a hospital ward and losing control of his empire. He worries about being crippled or having a stroke just as much as anyone else worries about these things. If you want to make someone feel uncomfortable and edgy in your presence then remind him that he is exposing himself to danger every time he eats red meat or drinks too much. If you want to make him feel unhappy and you want to make him dislike you then comment disapprovingly on his smoking habits and point out the number of people who die of lung cancer and heart disease caused by smoking. If, however, you want to make a big eating, heavy drinking executive like you then you should allay his fears and make him feel more comfortable by giving the impression that you're eating exactly the same sort of diet – and drinking the same amount of booze – as he is. And tell him how fit and well he looks.

Money

Money doesn't just mean possessions and luxuries – it means security and independence. And even the rich and apparently unassailable worry about money. The millionaire worries about losing his millions just as much as the man without a penny in the bank worries about how he is going to pay the electricity bill. It is sometimes said that the people who worry least about money are the people who have absolute huge quantities of it (and who have always had absolutely huge quantities of it) and the people who have absolutely none of it. The monk and the billionaire enjoy a certain freedom that the rest of us never really know. The man who has just bought a new house and who has a massive mortgage will worry more than he worried when he was living in a small house with a small mortgage. He will worry in case he loses his job. He will worry in case interest rates go up. Suddenly, things that are happening a thousand miles away seem important. A strike on the other side of the world may pose a real threat to his job and his security. A world wide recession keeps him awake at night. Most people worry about money because they never have quite enough of it – every time they get a little more money they raise their standards of living. The result is that instead of giving them extra security and freedom that little extra money has put them into a position where they need more money. Instead of being less vulnerable they become more vulnerable. The only people who achieve true contentment are the people who keep their standard of living comfortably below an income that they know they can rely on – and that is not dependent on any outside influences.

Such freedom is rare. Big companies know how vulnerable their employees are to financial worries and use simple techniques to use this knowledge to increase their power. For example, a company that wants to have complete control over its employees will selectively hire married men with responsibilities and families to look after. They will then loan these employees huge amounts of money to buy luxury homes and cars. And they will provide the loans at low interest rates. They know perfectly well that the employee is simply, effectively and permanently trapped by this arrangement. If the man's boss wants him to move to another city or spend six months in Argentina or take on an unpleasant responsibility he can make the suggestion confident in the knowledge that the employee is unlikely to have the courage to demur. The company will have bought the employee. On a much simpler level if you have men working on your house and you give them the agreed payment in advance then the chances are that they will work without enthusiasm. They will disappear for days at a time. Their work will be shoddy. They will be rude and aggressive. They have no clear incentive to please you. If, on the other hand, you pay them nothing in advance then they will work as speedily, as carefully and as courteously as they are able. To understand just how much an individual worries about money you need only to have a rough idea of his income and his outgoings. However confident that individual may seem he will have deep fears and anxieties if he is aware that his financial balance is a precarious one.

A lack of self-confidence

Most people lack real confidence in themselves. The man who has genuine, complete self-confidence is a rare beast. Usually, even the most aggressive, most forceful, most dominating individual will have inner doubts which will assail him from time to time. The man who seems brash and arrogant will be as susceptible to fear and anxiety as anyone. This self doubt and lack of self-confidence is usually inspired by guilt – an emotion that is difficult to define precisely but which is as common as love and as damaging as hate. Guilt is without a doubt one of the most powerful and damaging of human emotions. We torture ourselves with recriminations and then, having prosecuted ourselves, we find ourselves guilty. There are so many possible sources of guilt that it is impossible to classify them all. But most varieties of guilt fall into one of two main categories. First, there are the types of guilt that result from our personal relationships with other people. Sometimes guilt can be introduced crudely and deliberately as when a mother says to her son or daughter: 'You wouldn't do that if you loved me.' Sometimes guilt is produced subtly and unintentionally, as when one partner says to another: 'Don't worry about me, you go off and enjoy yourself. I'll be all right.' There are other types of guilt which result from the demands, expectations and teachings from those around us. Most of us have an inbuilt sense of right and wrong and if we trespass against it we feel guilty. All this guilt has a number of damaging effects but the most important and damaging effect it has is to create within us a feeling of inferiority and inadequacy; a real lack of self-confidence. We may cover this lack of confidence with a superficial polish and a glossy confidential air but underneath it there is agony and fear.

Remember that everyone has an inner weakness and a need for more confidence. By and large the brasher an individual the greater that internal need for reassurance. You can use this fact to your advantage in two simple and direct ways. First, you can build up the confidence of someone with whom you are working and you can, thereby, make him feel happier and more comfortable. He will like you when you tell him how wonderful he is. Even the greatest and most successful individual in the world needs to be reminded of his greatness and success. So remind him. Tell him what a wonderful person he is and what a marvellous job he is doing. Tell him confidentially, tell him with honesty in your voice and admiration in your eyes. He will feel warmly towards you. He will need to have you close to him. He will rely on you. If you work for him then he will promote you and pay you more money.

Second, of course, you can use an opponent's internal guilt and lack of self-confidence to control him and weaken him. Remind him constantly of his failures. Point out possible risks and dangers that lie ahead. Point out his weaknesses and remind him that he has enemies. Make a list of the people who don't like him. Make a list of his recognised faults. Remind him constantly of these faults. You don't need to be offensive or crude to do this. You can offer the information and advice in a helpful manner. Superficially you are offering constructive support. But deep down you are encouraging him to destroy himself with a feeling of inferiority and a lack of self-confidence.

Ignorance

No one likes to be thought ignorant or stupid. Everyone likes to be thought of as bright, well informed and well educated. Most of us fall somewhere between these two extremes. We are not entirely ignorant. But we don't know everything. (I write in general terms and naturally you and I are exempt from this rule.) What makes us anxious is the knowledge that we have weaknesses – there are subjects about which we know very little. We worry in case our ignorance is exposed in public and we are made to look gauche, ill informed or just plain stupid. You can use this fear to help you manage your relationships with others in two ways.

First, of course, you must get an idea of the sort of areas of weakness that your opponent has. You must find out what he knows a little about and what he knows very little about. Once you have that basic information you will be free to control and manipulate his behaviour. If you want to get him to like you and enjoy your company, talk about the sort of things he knows a lot about. If he is a keen yachtsman and an expert fly fisherman, talk about boats and fly fishing. It doesn't matter if you know little or nothing. All you have to do is to ask simple questions that encourage him to keep talking. He will feel good about showing off his knowledge. And, as a pleasant side effect you will be gaining new information and, maybe, filling in another gap in your knowledge. A word of warning: even if you are knowledgeable in the area concerned don't say too much, resist the temptation to show off your knowledge. If you show that you are too well informed then you will devalue your opponent's knowledge. He will not feel so confident. He will not feel so superior. And he will not like you so much.

If, on the other hand, you want to make your opponent feel small, incompetent and gauche then you should try to keep the conversation concentrated on subjects about which he knows very little – making sure, of course, that it is a subject about which you know a great deal. So, for example, if you know that he knows very little about wine but you know quite a lot about wine then talk incessantly about wines! Take every opportunity to expose his ignorance. Talk to him about vintages and about vineyards. Ask him questions. Ask his opinion. If possible ask him for information and advice in company where his ignorance will be exposed more cruelly. Your opponent will, of course, grow to hate you and to fear you. He will not enjoy your company. If you are clever and subtle about the way you do it then he probably won't really know why but he will not like being with you. When he knows that he is going to meet you his heart will beat a little faster and he will feel acid pouring into his stomach. His muscles will grow tense and he will probably develop a headache. Eventually the mere mention of your name will make him feel ill. You will have established a clear sense of superiority. (Though beware: do this to your boss and he'll probably sack you.)

Sex

He may not think much about sex. He may not worry at all about sex. But sex is a strange subject. And it is ridiculously easy to make anyone worry about his sexual feelings, his sexual successes, his sexual powers and his sexual interests. All you have to do is to imply that his sexual interests and achievements or hopes or aspirations are in some way abnormal. Most of the people you meet will have hang-ups about sex – though they may not be aware of those hang-ups. They will have repressions and fears and hidden anxieties. You can easily expose those hidden repressions, fears and anxieties by suggesting (quite subtly and tactfully, of course) that his desires are in some way abnormal. You can suggest that if he were normal he would be thinking more about sex. You can suggest that he is unusual because he doesn't share what you suggest is a widely held penchant for a particular sexual activity. You can suggest that he is abnormal – and may need treatment – because he does have a desire for some particular perversion. You can imply that his abilities to perform are in question. The list of possibilities is endless.

After a business dinner you can take him to a nightclub where his actions will inevitably put him in a weak position. If he takes advantage of the sexual delights that are on offer he is exhibiting weaknesses. If, on the other hand, he refuses the sexual delights that are offered then he may feel that he is exposing himself as something less than a man. (What you would do in those circumstances would be to make your excuses and leave – having hinted that you have made your own, very personal arrangements but that you do not want to mix business with pleasure. He, not having read this book, will merely be confused, frightened and alarmed.)

Appearance

We all worry about the way we look. Huge industries have been built up with the solitary aim of selling us products and services that are designed to help us improve our appearances. These days men are as vulnerable to these fears as are women. Millions are spent by men on cosmetic surgery and on cosmetics. Businessmen as well as pop singers spend money getting rid of unwanted bags under their eyes and acquiring expensive looking sun tans. Whatever their sex people worry about the shape of their bodies, their weight, their hair and their skin colour. Women worry about the size and shape of their breasts and bottoms. Men worry about the size and shape of their sexual organs. Women worry about their thighs. Men worry about their bottoms. Women worry about their hair colour. Men worry about the amount of hair they have (or have not) got. Women worry about their eyebrows. Both sexes worry about their mouths, their noses and the number of chins they have. These fears are genuine, deep rooted and common place. More superficially, but of equal importance, men and women worry about their clothes and their accessories. Women worry about their dresses and their jewellery. Men worry about their suits, shirts and ties. Both sexes worry that their clothes look crumpled, badly cared for or cheap.

These anxieties are easily soothed or enhanced. To soothe someone's fears (and to make him feel more comfortable and content) you merely have to offer modest but genuine congratulations on his appearance. He will take an instant liking to you. If, on the other hand, you make some mildly disparaging remark such as 'You've put on some weight, haven't you?' or 'Still got the old favourite suit I see?' then you'll make him feel desperately uncomfortable. He'll dislike you and probably be a little afraid of you.

Friends and relatives

Everyone loves to be loved. Everyone loves to feel that he has lots of friends and that his relatives all love him dearly. But few people are really confident that they do have enough friends or that their relatives do really love them quite enough. Most of the people you meet – either socially or through business – will feel guilty about the way they've treated someone. They will be conscious of the fact that they don't visit their parents often enough. They will feel that they should have written a letter to a friend or a relative who called or wrote months ago.

You can use this natural and widespread fear to your advantage. If you want to make someone feel edgy and slightly uncomfortable then try to drop into your conversation the names of lots of friends. They don't have to be famous or important friends (in fact it is better if they aren't – simple name dropping can be counter productive). The aim is simply to let the other person know that you have lots of friends and are therefore, by definition, a likeable person. The person you are talking to will admire you and respect you and will feel slightly inferior and inadequate. The impact of your offensive can be made that much greater by your hinting strongly that these are all true friends who would always be willing to help you in times of need. Give the impression that your friends are loyal, kind, generous and honourable. Say something like, 'A real friend is someone who'd get out of bed at 3 in the morning to drive 300 miles and pick you up from the other end of the country, don't you think?' The person you are talking to will have to agree. Deep down he'll probably have difficulty in thinking of anyone he knows who would be prepared to do such a thing. You then say, 'Of course, I don't suppose any of us have more than a dozen real friends who'd satisfy that sort of definition.' He then feels terribly lonely. You've exposed him to his own hidden, secret fear. His personal weakness is staring him in the face. He isn't really a very nice person. Not many people really like him. He hasn't got many real friends. At the same time he will feel tremendous respect for you. You will, quite speedily and easily, have manipulated the situation so that you are in control.

A meaningful life

Everyone has dreams. At eighteen we all want to do something with our lives. We want to make our mark. We want to do something that will bring us fame, fortune and respect. We want to be remembered. We want to change the world or create an empire that will last long after we have become ashes. We want to create a work of art, paint a masterpiece, write a great novel or build a wonderful cathedral. We want to represent our country at sport. We want to become political leaders. We want to be rewarded and praised for our courage and bravery. Sadly, of course, by the time we reach twenty most of those dreams have been lost or abandoned. We settle down and accept our limitations. We dreamt of fame and fortune but we settle for a job as regional sales manager and a small house in the suburbs. We dreamt of changing the world and being internationally respected. We settle for a new car every two years and a key to the executive washroom. These lost dreams are universal. The shop assistant who snottily refuses you credit once had dreams of her own. The employer who gives you a tough interview when you're applying for a job once dreamt of being an international tycoon. The solicitor who greedily overcharges while helping you buy your house probably had a dream of improving the world. When we start off we believe that our lives are going to be special and meaningful. By the time we reach early middle age we are ready to accept that we have to readjust our aim; we have to set our sights a little lower and be a touch more realistic.

If you are in conflict with someone you can use their lost dreams to help you gain the upper hand. To achieve this you must do two things. First, you must make it clear to them that you have not lost *your* dreams. You must make it clear that you still have high hopes and aspirations. You must make it clear that your dreams are still intact. You must talk about your hopes and your aspirations. You must make it clear that your life still has real meaning.

Second, you must make the person with whom you are in conflict come to face the fact that he has lost his dreams. You must ask him to tell you his hopes and his ambitions. You must encourage him to talk about the hopes he had when he was eighteen. He will probably talk freely and with some enthusiasm about these lost aims. Whatever initial shyness and diffidence there is will soon be lost – people love talking about themselves. If you nod with encouragement then he will soon get to like you. He will find your interest and enthusiasm attractive. But slowly, maybe later when he is sitting in his car on the way home or when he is lying in bed or in the bath, he will be haunted by those old, previously forgotten dreams. He will suddenly become dissatisfied with his life. He will realise how shallow are his aims and ambitions. He will feel disappointed, thwarted and frustrated. He will remember those early dreams with happiness. His life will suddenly seem dull, meaningless and purposeless. He will feel aggrieved and ashamed.

At this point the person you are in conflict with will become receptive to new ideas and unusually eager to take chances. His outlook on life will change quite dramatically and the outcome of your negotiations with him will probably change too.

Boredom and worry

When a large group of people was asked to say what worried them two unusual and rather unexpected replies came high up on the list. An astonishingly high number of people confessed that they worried about being bored – and that they did not like not having enough to do. And an almost equal number of people said that they were simply worried that they worried too much!

These two fears are, it seems, extremely common. Both men and women admit that they hate the idea of life without any purpose and men and women of all ages confess that they worry far too much about trivial matters over which they have no control. You can, quite easily, use these natural and widespread fears to help you strengthen a negotiating position. First, you can draw these fears out into the open. Talk about them. Get your opponent to think of these problems and to concentrate on his own attitude towards both anxieties. Get him to recognise that he too is frightened of finding himself without enough to do. Ask him how he plans to spend his retirement. Ask him to tell you how he would spend his days if he were suddenly to be made redundant. Then ask him what sort of things make him worry. Ask him, indeed, if he would describe himself as a worrier. Point out sympathetically that all the evidence shows that people who worry are most likely to suffer from stress related disorders.

He will then worry even more – and worry about worrying. You will have manipulated your opponent into a position of weakness.

Warning

Remember that everyone you meet will, in practice, be a number of different people! We all automatically adapt our attitudes and actions to suit the people we are with. We act differently with our competitors, lovers, spouses, employers, neighbours, doctors, friends and relatives. A middle aged, divorced man working as an executive in a large company may be generous and loving with his children, bitter towards his ex-wife, sycophantic towards his managing director, lustful towards his secretary, respectful to his parents, frightened of his dentist and hungry for success. His children may be frightened of him, his former wife may be jealous of his freedom, his managing director may regard his humility as a sign of insecurity and inferiority, his secretary may be excited by his advances but loyal to her husband, his parents may be proud of him and his dentist may be bored by him.

In each relationship that any of us has there are a number of different driving forces. A man whose car has been stolen will be angry with the thief, guilty about having forgotten to lock the car door and anxious about his wife's reaction. A woman who has been sacked will be angry with her employer, depressed about her inability to hold down a job and concerned about her children who may suffer because of the shortage of money that will result. In any situation the emotions we feel and the actions we take result directly from the combination of driving forces we experience. We may be aware of some of those forces but many of them will not arouse any conscious action.

In offices and factories, shops and hospitals, you can watch people changing personality all the time. People will change according to the person they're meeting and they will change because of their inner feelings, aspirations, fears and ambitions.

You may think you know your partner but you only know what he – or she – is with you. What about when he is with other people?

See him with his boss and he'll probably be less confident, quieter and surprisingly diffident. See him with his pals in a club and he'll be rowdy, brash and sure of himself. See him with a cashier in the canteen and he'll be saucy. All this is made even more complicated by the fact that if he knows you are watching him then his behaviour will be changed yet again.

The result is that different people see your partner in very different ways. And the reason is simple: your partner isn't just one person. He is a crowd of people crammed into one body.

The same thing is true of everyone else you know. Your best friend is many different people. So is your mother. And your father. Your neighbour may be regarded as bad tempered and aggressive by some people but as charming and considerate by others.

Look around. Get to understand the ways in which the people you know change their responses according to the people they are with.

How to be a successful interviewee

I can still remember the first job interview I ever attended. I turned up, dressed in my one and only suit, and joined the queue of nervous short-listed applicants. Anxious not to ruin my chances by turning up late I got there a good half an hour early and by the time my name was called I was well on the way to a full blooded panic attack. As I walked towards the interview room I had to wipe my sweaty palms on my trousers so that I didn't blow my chances at the first handshake.

Taking a few, slow deep breaths to calm my beating heart I took hold of the door knob with my right hand, knocked with my left and, upon hearing a distant call of 'Come' walked briskly and confidently into the room. I walked straight into a large wooden table that had been placed just inside the door.

It was only several years later that I began to suspect that the interviewers had put that table there to discomfort would-be employees. My guess is that they knew very well that everyone coming into the room would walk straight into it and lose both composure and confidence.

In retrospect it was one of my first lessons in life. Interviews are battles and there are no rules. There is no Geneva convention to protect interviewees.

Although interview techniques have come quite a long way since then – and have become far more sophisticated – the general principles remain very much the same. The interviewer has a limited amount of time in which to find out as much as he can about you. In order to persuade you to reveal your inner thoughts, fears, feelings, ambitions and fantasies he will resort to all sorts of little tricks. Whether you are attending a job interview, an interview that might lead to a promotion or an interview for a college place the interviewer (or interviewers) will have been trained to look at the way you behave and the way you answer questions as much as to the answers you give.

You should not, however, let any of this discourage you.

It isn't difficult to learn how to play the interview game. With a little thought and preparation you can influence your chances of impressing the interviewer(s) and attaining your objective.

Here, then, are my suggestions for winning at interviews.

1. Do your homework

Find out what the interviewers are likely to be looking for – and how you can supply their need. Telephone a clerk or secretary and try to find out who will be conducting the interview. Then try to learn as much as you can about their personal preferences and prejudices. See if you can find their name in a local Who's Who directory. Do some research about the organisation they represent. Get hold of a copy of the Annual Report. Collect any promotional material that you can get hold of (so that you show that you have done your research and that you know a little about the company or organisation you'll be asking to join).

Check out the company dress style and code. There is no point at all in turning up to an interview wearing jeans and a sweat shirt if all employees are expected to wear a dark suit and a white shirt. You will simply antagonise the interviewer and lose marks before you sit down. But remember that you must dress in something in which you feel reasonably relaxed. If you feel good then you'll look good. Try not to wear something new and uncomfortable – if you do then the chances are that you will look as uncomfortable and as edgy as you feel. And make sure that you find out about any special personal or sporting skills or achievements that the interviewer may have. A friend of mine once applied for a job at a large factory and boasted proudly of his skills as a footballer in the local amateur side. He found out two days later that the dull old fool in the blue blazer who had said nothing during the interview had been a national hero thirty years earlier and had played football for his country. Another friend boasted of his home wine making skills and subsequently discovered that one member of the interview board owned a vineyard in France.

2. Build up your self-confidence

Interviewers don't like assertive, over-confident applicants. But they don't like people who have no confidence either. You need to acquire (or at least learn to fake) a quiet, deep, inner confidence in yourself. Start by making a list of all your virtues and qualities. Pretend that you're an advertising agency preparing a campaign designed to 'sell' yourself to the world. Every time you feel nervous or frightened remind yourself of your imaginary advertising campaign.

Add to your sense of confidence by using your imagination. Twice a day spend a few minutes trying to 'see' yourself at your interview. Imagine yourself coping with and charming the interviewer. Imagine him as a cruel, hard and vicious beast. (That way he will almost certainly turn out to be better than you expect). Imagine yourself succeeding. If you constantly 'see' yourself failing to impress then you'll end up very nervous and you'll probably make a mess of things. Your prophecy will be self fulfilling. If you constantly 'see' yourself succeeding then you'll be much more likely to succeed. Finally, remember that the interviewers want you to be a success just as much as you want to be a success. They need you. That is why they are conducting the interview. They have to find someone to fill an empty job or take an empty college place. The interviewer is not trying to make you look a fool or trying to fail you. The interviewer is merely trying to find the best person for the job. Strange though it may seem the interviewer really wants you to be the best candidate in the entire world. It will make his life much easier if there is one candidate who is so good that he automatically picks himself.

3. Decide what you want

If you're going for a job interview, for example, decide in advance what working conditions you're prepared to accept. Will you do shift work? Will you work away from home? What is the lowest salary you're prepared to accept? Do you want a company car? How much holiday do you want? If you don't ask yourself these questions in advance you will probably end up looking a fool (for not knowing the answers) or else you'll end up with a bad deal. Either way you lose.

4. Prepare for the worst

Having already told you to be confident I know that this sounds crazy. But it makes sense. If you go to an interview believing that your whole life depends on the interview being successful then you'll end up so nervous that you'll probably make a mess of things. Spend a little time deciding what you'll do if things don't work out. Make alternative, positive plans for the future. You'll probably be surprised to find out that there are other things you'd quite like to do. And because it isn't quite so vital you won't be so nervous when you go for the interview. One of the ironies of life is that if you don't really have to have a job then you'll stand a much better chance of getting it. If you are too desperate you'll try too hard and you'll fail.

5. Present yourself properly

If you were trying to sell a car you'd try to make it look smart, wouldn't you? You'd clean out the sweet wrappers and empty cola tins and you'd clean the paintwork. So do your best to make yourself look clean, neat and attractive.

The interviewer knows that what he sees is you at your best. He'll probably never see you looking as smart ever again. When you go to an interview you're trying to sell yourself. So package and present yourself carefully and thoughtfully. Do not, however, keep a special interview suit. If you do then the chances are that the suit will be so heavy with nervous memories that you'll start to feel edgy just as soon as you put it on. Remember your shoes. It may be illogical and unfair but interviewers are often put off by grubby shoes.

6. Beware of tricks

The interview doesn't start when you start talking. It starts the minute you go in through the front door of the building where the interview will take place. If you've parked your car in their car park it starts there. I know of someone who conducts interviews in the ante room pretending to be a window cleaner. When applicants go into the interview room they see an assistant. The interview is over by then. Remember that the secretary or receptionist out front may well have more power or influence than you think. And remember what I said earlier: interviews are war. There are no rules.

7. Smile

Don't crack jokes. The interviewer may not have a sense of humour. He may not like your jokes. He may be offended. He may not appreciate the idea of an employee who wastes time telling jokes. But do smile. Go in with a smile on your face and try to leave with a smile on your face. We all feel more comfortable with people who smile occasionally (though not an idiot, fixed, synchronised swimming type of grin). Interviewers are no exception. The interviewer will respond to your smile just as well as anyone else will.

8. Relax yourself

Take deep, slow breaths before you go in to calm your beating heart and settle your breathing pattern. Wiggle and stretch your fingers and toes. And run your tongue over your teeth and gums. All these simple physical actions will help you to relax. If you can then try daydreaming while you're waiting to go in. Imagine that you're somewhere peaceful and relaxing – on a holiday beach maybe.

9. Don't be a creep

You may find this difficult to believe but most interviewers aren't stupid. If you want to influence the interviewer, you must avoid insulting his intelligence. Don't insist that you want to work for Asbestos Knickers International plc because you've always wanted to get into the asbestos knicker industry and have dreamt of working for Asbestos Knickers International plc since you were six. He won't believe you. Tell him you've heard that the company is growing – and you want to be a part of that growth. Tell him you think the company's past performance is impressive.

10. Sparkle

As an interviewee you're on stage. The interviewer is your audience. Try to make eye contact. Never stop to explain unless you are asked to. Don't be defensive. Don't be hesitant. Never ramble. Don't be negative. Be brisk, business-like and – above all – remember to sparkle. When child actress Shirley Temple was on the film set for hour after hour she began to wilt. So her manager would remind her to 'sparkle' when the cameras began to roll. You need to remember the same thing. The interviewer is probably tired and bored and, quite possibly, wishes he was somewhere else. But he already has a job. You've got to make him like you. Stay alert, interested and enthusiastic.

Look at him when you talk. Try to look into his eyes – if you do, your eyes will sparkle. If you concentrate on his eyes, your pupils will enlarge and he'll know (subconsciously) that you find him interesting. Subconsciously he'll be flattered. Once you've made him feel flattered by your presence you're more than half way there.

How to negotiate successfully

Negotiations are an essential and integral part of business and politics. In every negotiation there are times when you must be firm and times when you must compromise.

Here are my tips on how to negotiate successfully.

⚜ Before you start remember that every partner in a negotiation has hopes and desires. You are unlikely to get everything you want. Any negotiation will eventually become a compromise. The best you can expect from a business opponent is enlightened selfishness.

⚜ Try to find out what your opponent really wants. What he wants may be very different from what he says he wants.

⚜ Try to make sure that your opponent understands what *you* really want. Outline your main aims and proposals and establish early on any areas where you aren't prepared to compromise.

⚜ The real power in any negotiation lies with the individual who is prepared to walk away. So before you start decide at what point you would break off negotiations and walk away. Decide what you would do. Decide what is the worst deal you would accept. And make sure that the person with whom you are negotiating believes that you *will* walk away from the negotiating table if necessary.

❦ Try to discover any time limits under which your opponent is operating. And try to make your time scale longer than his. For example, if you find that your opponent has to finish the negotiations within two weeks (because of some instructions outside his control) but you can delay a decision for four weeks, then you are in a very strong position. You can mess around for the first twelve days. By then your opponent will be getting very edgy. He knows that he is running out of time. He will be getting panicky. You will have a distinct advantage.

❦ Develop a fall back position. Set up alternatives – things that you can do if the negotiations break down completely.

❦ If you are negotiating as part of a team make sure that each member of the team knows his role. The worst thing any negotiating team can do is argue publicly in front of their opponents. So make sure that one individual is given authority as spokesman. Another member of the team should be given the job of making notes and trying to assess the main claims and demands of the opposition. A third team member should offer to be secretary and to record all observations and conclusions. If someone from your team is preparing the final report then you cannot lose. The other side will object if his report is biased or unfair or does not reasonably represent the conclusions drawn by the two sides. But you will undoubtedly be able to win some extra negotiating points if you are in charge of the report writing. So, for example, if the report writer misinterprets four points in your favour you should be able to retain at least one of those misinterpretations in the subsequent post report negotiations.

❦ Try to define rules, regulations, expectations and

assumptions before you start. Otherwise your opponent may be working to different rules. You could be in for a terrible shock at the end of the negotiations if you don't know exactly what you're talking about before you start.

❀ Remember the power of silence. TV interviewers use this tool regularly. When an interviewee has apparently stopped talking the interviewer will wait and say nothing. Embarrassed by the silence and eager to satisfy the interviewer's obvious need for more the interviewee will ramble on, invariably giving away secrets and confidential comments that he would otherwise not have shared with anyone – let alone a television camera. You can use this power of silence across the negotiating table. Say nothing and your opponents will feel obliged to fill the silence.

❀ If you are negotiating on the telephone use the technology to your advantage. So, for example, if you want time to think hang up the telephone in mid sentence – as though you have been cut off. This will give you time to think. Then keep your phone off the hook for a couple of minutes before redialling. Your opponent will undoubtedly be trying to ring you and it will take him a while to realise that if he's going to speak to you again he'll have to put his phone down and wait for you to get through – he will have assumed that your phone is engaged because you are trying to call him.

❀ Don't be frightened of using 'dirty tricks' when negotiating. Remember: only losers fight fair. For example, lead your opponent deep into negotiations – so that he invests a good deal of time and effort on them. Then, just as you are about to make an agreement demand one last concession. If you aren't careful this can appear to be a grasping, vulgar, undignified negotiating ploy – but it often works. It is frequently used by some of the world's most successful businessmen. On the other hand if you suspect that your opponent is using dirty tricks to gain the upper hand don't be afraid to expose him. But do it in an innocent way – making it clear that you aren't a fool but not making future negotiations difficult. Use your opponent's dirty tricks to make him feel small and rather embarrassed. Say something sweet like: 'Could we have some blinds fitted for tomorrow – the sun is in my eyes. For now perhaps we could move our chairs around a little?' Your opponent, who has deliberately put you in a position where you are blinded by the sun, will feel uncomfortable but you will have made your point easily, tactfully and effectively.

How to manage people successfully

Being a boss isn't all perks and business lunches. There are problems galore. When people work for you then you are responsible for them. You can make them feel comfortable or uncomfortable, happy or miserable. You can ensure that they enjoy their work and you can make life terrible for them. You can encourage them to stay when they could get more money and better conditions elsewhere and you can force them to leave even though they're moving to a poorer paid job.

To manage people successfully you have somehow to ensure that you get the best out of them while at the same time keeping them happy.

Here is some advice on how you can balance these two objectives.

1. Say 'thank you'
Not long ago I attended a massive, international conference. It was a huge success. Delegates had flown in from all

over the world and they were delighted with the arrangements. The lectures were informative and useful. The food was delicious. The evening entertainments were well planned and brilliantly and imaginatively executed. The hotel accommodation was excellent. A fairly junior executive had worked day and night for six months to ensure that everything was a success. His marriage had been put under an extraordinary strain.

On the last evening of the conference I found the junior executive in a dark corner of the hotel bar. He was alone and quietly getting drunk.

When I asked him what the matter was and why he wasn't joining in the final evening celebrations he told me that he was thinking of leaving his company – even though he had an excellent job and a generous salary. He said he never ever wanted to see the company chairman again.

Knowing that the directors had been extremely pleased with the executive's work – and that they all felt that the conference had been a great success – I was rather surprised. I asked him why he felt so low.

'I've just been give my next assignment,' the executive sobbed into his brandy. 'It's a good job I guess. But do you know, I've just put six months of my life into this conference and I didn't even get a "thank you"?'

That was what was hurting.

No one had said 'thank you' or 'well done'.

The message is that you can give a man a better job; you can give him a pay rise; you can give him a bigger car, a posher office or more secretaries. But nothing replaces a quiet, honest, old fashioned 'thank you'.

People like to know that the boss cares and is pleased. People like to be reminded that they are doing a good job.

2. Give people as much responsibility as they can handle

Over promoting employees – and giving them too much responsibility – causes many problems. But giving employees too little responsibility can also cause problems.

An American telephone company in a large town employed a dozen women to prepare telephone directories for publication. The women all worked together on the whole project, sharing the general responsibility for the work they were doing. The directories were full of errors – subscribers' names omitted, names spelt wrongly – and there were numerous complaints.

Then someone had a brainwave. Each woman was given direct responsibility for producing an individual telephone directory. Each woman became 'editor' of her 'own' telephone book.

The improvement was staggering. The number of mistakes in each directory fell dramatically. The turnover of staff also fell. And the number of days lost through sickness dropped.

The work hadn't changed at all. But by dividing it up in a different way, and sharing the responsibility individually rather than collectively, efficiency improved considerably.

By and large the more responsibility you give people the more responsible they will be.

3. Don't underestimate the peril of boredom

A car manufacturer once claimed that people never want to think at work. He used to encourage his employees to hang up their minds in the cloakroom.

He was wrong. He didn't understand people very well at all.

Repetitive, boring, routine work causes errors, inefficiency, disputes, absenteeism and ill health. It is often boredom that drives people to drink too much or to take mind bending drugs.

And yet despite the existence of the evidence showing the problems associated with boredom there are millions of people around today whose work demands nothing more than that they act as nursemaids to expensive, complicated pieces of machinery which they do not understand. In factories there are pieces of machinery which can turn out finely finished objects no craftsmen working with his own hands and tools could hope to copy. In offices there are computers and word processors which can write letters, check spelling and keep files far more speedily and efficiently than any individual could. These days machines are so sophisticated that they too often become the principals in any working relationship. The individual is, too often, left too little opportunity to show pride or self expression.

To counteract this problem – and to combat the peril of boredom – you should:

☑ Ensure that repetitive or monotonous tasks are spread around as much as possible.

☑ Always try to design jobs with people in mind. Remember that people are a basic and essential resource. If you use people properly then you will make better and more efficient use of your other resources.

☑ Look for new ways to add responsibility to people's lives – remember that an industrial rut can easily become a slough of despond.

☑ Try to get rid of assembly lines – foreign car companies have shown that product quality goes up, absenteeism goes down and productivity rises when assembly lines are disassembled and workers are divided into groups and given the responsibility for producing individual vehicles.

☑ Never employ anyone solely to 'mind' a machine. People must always know that they are more important than the machines they work with – machines should be introduced to make jobs easier or more efficient. Remember that the man, not the machine, is the principal partner in any relationship.

4. Teach people that it's OK to say 'No'

'No' is one of the most difficult words to say in the English language. Not being able to say 'no' leads us into all sorts of difficult and painful, personal circumstances. It results in commitments we can't cope with, dinner parties that are a real bore and unwanted pregnancies. It leads to your company being committed to projects and partners which are neither suitable nor profitable. It leads to agreements and contracts which prove embarrassing and costly. And it leads to people buying materials that are substandard or not needed.

People say 'yes' when they should say 'no' for all sorts of reasons.

People say 'yes' because they have been blackmailed; because they are vain and want to appear strong and decisive; because they are too frightened or embarrassed to say 'no' and because they want to please the person who wants them to say 'yes'.

You should teach your employees that there is nothing wrong with saying 'no' occasionally.

5. Teach employees to ask for help

Many people feel that asking for help is a sign of weakness. This is a great pity.

By asking for help, advice and information we can all help ourselves and one another.

The message you must get across is that knowing when to ask for help (and being prepared to ask for help) is a sign of strength not weakness. Knowing whom to ask for help (and knowing what questions to ask) is a sign of wisdom not ignorance.

6. Put purpose into people's lives

Once upon a time there were two bricklayers. They both did exactly the same work for the same local builder.

The first bricklayer found his work extremely tedious. 'All I do every day is lay one brick on top of another,' he complained. 'My only moment of satisfaction is when I pick up my wage packet on a Friday afternoon.'

That bricklayer was for ever off work – usually complaining of vague physical symptoms. But his real complaint was that he had no enthusiasm for his work. To him it seemed purposeless.

The second bricklayer enjoyed his work. 'I build houses,' he said proudly. 'Every day I think of the people who will occupy the house I'm building and who will turn it into a home. I think of their excitement. I think of their children. I think of the generations who will see what I have helped to create.'

This bricklayer was hardly ever away from work. His life had purpose and meaning.

7. Don't fuss

Once you have given someone responsibility try not to interfere too much. Don't become a fusspot.

Remember that too many rules, too many meetings and too many reports will cost money, ruin efficiency and destroy the morale of the people who should be doing the work. Sending a stream of memos and reminders to a senior manager is like reminding a 40-year-old to put on a clean vest and pick up a fresh handkerchief every morning.

8. Encourage employees to show their anger

Anger is one of the commonest, most fundamental and most damaging of human emotions. It is inspired by thoughtlessness, indifference and officiousness. It can be produced by frustration, disappointment or a real or imagined injustice.

Whatever the cause may be anger can be physically, mentally, socially and economically damaging. Stored, suppressed anger produces high blood pressure, stomach ulceration, heart disease and all the other symptoms of stress induced disease.

In order to reduce the damaging effects of anger you should try to encourage your employees to express their anger.

First, try to ensure that there are pathways for protest within your organisation.

Second, provide some facilities where employees can get rid of their accumulated tensions and anger. Hitting a tennis ball or squash ball or kicking a football around can all help employees get rid of their aggression (assuming that they are fit enough and healthy enough to exercise, of course).

Finally, remember that anger is a perfectly natural and reasonably healthy response to stressful circumstances. Everyone gets angry from time to time and suppressing anger – or refusing to acknowledge its existence – can be dangerous.

Remember, people only get angry because they care. By showing that you care too, their anger will do less damage.

9. Make the most of other people's skills

Jane worked for a large insurance company as a senior secretary. But she was bored. She did her job well enough but it wasn't much of a challenge. Her real love was writing. In her spare time she wrote a weekly column for the local newspaper. They didn't pay her very much but she enjoyed it. Gradually, as the months went by, she started to spend more and more time writing and less and less time being a secretary. Her boss caught her writing articles in his time. But he didn't want to lose her. Even on half power she was worth her money. And then he had a brainwave. For some time he had been thinking of introducing a small, quarterly company newsletter for members of staff, shareholders and some of the company's bigger customers. He'd originally planned to bring in someone from outside to be the part time editor. But then he had the idea of offering the job to Jane. She was thrilled. She put her heart and soul into her new job. And the newsletter was a tremendous success. She even took more pride and interest in her work as a secretary.

Some people would have sacked Jane. Others would have merely put up with an inefficient and bored secretary. Jane's boss managed to get the best of both worlds. He retained an excellent employee and found a way to use her talents to the company's best advantage. Everyone was happy.

Remember: a fancy peg is wasted in a square hole.

10. Show people that you're interested in them

Really good salesmen carry a small card index around with them. When they arrive at a client's they will stop for a moment and pick out the relevant entry. Then they will refresh their memories about the client. They'll remind themselves that he has a wife and two children called Samantha and Jason. They'll find the date of the client's birthday and wedding anniversary (previously obtained from a chatty secretary). They'll rediscover that he's a keen tennis player and that he suffers from high blood pressure. They'll be reminded of his favourite food, drink and type of holiday. They'll know about his politics and religion. Only when they are armed with all this information will they go in to see the client. They won't necessarily use all this information, of course. But it's there. And it can be used to make the client feel relaxed, loved and important.

At the end of the call the client will feel good. He'll be pleased to have seen a 'friend' who remembered his name, his birthday and his interests. He'll feel flattered that the salesman remembered that he went to Spain for his holidays last year. He'll feel liked and so he'll like the salesman. He'll probably buy from him.

Although this system works incredibly well for salesmen, managers and executives hardly ever use it to improve their relationship with their employees. The fact is, however, that if you let your employees know you are interested in them, they will be more loyal, they will work harder and they will be more enthusiastic about working for you and the company.

How to survive on the street

The way you behave on the street can decide whether or not you get mugged. In an experiment conducted in New York a hidden video camera was used to film a wide variety of men and women walking down the same street. The film was then shown to groups of convicted muggers. The prisoners all agreed on which people they would choose to mug.

They did not select individuals by age, race, sex or looks. It was the way that people walked and moved and behaved that determined their fate.

So, if you want to reduce your chances of being mugged here are some things you should remember:

☞ Walk at a good pace – sticking out your elbows. Try to walk in the funny, staccato way that people walk in old fashioned black and white silent movies.

☞ Wave occasionally as though you've seen a friend, a

shopkeeper you know or noticed a relative in an apartment window overlooking the street.

☞ If you can act crazy then do so. Muggers don't like crazies – they are too unpredictable. Try talking to yourself as you walk.

☞ Try to look as tall and as broad as you can. Stick out your chest, push back your shoulders and hold your head high. Look like a physical winner rather than a loser. Don't shuffle along with your head down.

☞ If you're walking through a dark or dodgy neighbourhood walk in the centre of the road – away from any possible ambush.

☞ If you see someone who could be a mugger don't look at him. If you look at someone you're challenging him – and he'll probably respond. If you have to pass a group of potential muggers try to walk past as though you haven't seen them. Don't respond and don't allow yourself to be annoyed into commenting.

☞ Try to look as much of a mess as you can. If you regularly drive and then park a motor car in streets where muggings often take place, don't clean it. If you're dressed in evening wear put an old coat on top if you have to walk through a dangerous area. Muggers are quickly influenced by superficial appearances.

☞ Take special care when crossing roads, getting out of or into a car or coming out of or into your home. It is at those times – when you are concentrating hard – that you are particularly vulnerable to muggers.

☞ If you are approached by someone who looks like a mugger don't stop to fight or argue. You'll almost certainly lose. Do two things: run as fast as you can and make as much noise as you can.

☞ Try to look relaxed and at ease. If you are walking tensely or nervously through a dangerous district then you will attract muggers like a jam pot attracts wasps. Try to look cool and confident and the muggers will probably decide to give you a miss.

How to manage your boss

Managing your boss need not be as difficult as you might imagine. Remember your boss is human – and vulnerable to the same fears and anxieties as everyone else.

Here are my tips on how best you can manage your boss.

∞ If you find your boss frightening then never, ever let him see that you are afraid. Never forget that he is a human being – just like you. If you begin to find yourself worrying about him, spend a few minutes every hour thinking of him in a vulnerable, exposed or embarrassing position. Think of him in the bath. Think of him being given a rectal examination by his doctor. Think of him sitting on the lavatory. Think of him being told off by his mother. Think of him sitting on a bedpan. Think of him having an enema. Think of him running to catch a plane or a train. Think of him being smacked as a child. Think of him in a subservient position to you.

∞ Try to study the way your boss thinks and acts. Find out what rattles him. Look for his strengths and his weaknesses. Try to imagine what his personal fears are. Try to remember that he too almost certainly has a boss (even if it is only the shareholders or a nagging spouse). Watch how he treats people. The more you know about your boss the better you will be able to deal with him.

∞ Never go to your boss with a problem unless you have

at least one and preferably three solutions ready to offer him. Most bosses are busy. They hate having new problems put on their desk. They love people who bring them answers and solutions. If you turn up with some answers to the problems you're bringing then your boss will like you and will probably give you extra responsibility (and you will have the pleasure of knowing that you are controlling what happens – you will have acquired some power).

🕭 Remember that because your boss is human he too likes to be praised and have his ego bolstered. But don't simply be sycophantic: that will get you nowhere. Try to find specific things that you can praise enthusiastically and honestly. If you really can't think of anything he does that is worth praising, look for things about the company, firm or partnership that you can praise.

🕭 If your boss is a bully let him know, firmly but politely, that you don't like taking nonsense from anyone. But don't shout back. However much he pushes you or tempts you try to remain calm. Think of him as an obnoxious schoolboy who is having a tantrum. If you know that he always likes to pick an argument, deliberately prepare an area where he can attack you – but be thoroughly prepared so that he can't win. He'll get the bullying out of his system but he'll respect you.

🕭 If your boss asks you to do something that you consider unacceptable or unethical ask him to repeat it. Get his suggestion in writing if you can. Or get it on tape. Or get a witness. Say you understand exactly what he is asking you to do. Then go away and ignore him completely. Do whatever you think is right. If you've made a poor judgement – and your boss is right – you'll probably lose your job but keep your self respect. If you've made a good judgement – and your boss was wrong – you'll keep your self respect and you may well get his job too.

⚭ If your boss is, quite simply, incompetent, try to establish good communications with other people in your organisation. Make sure that you get the credit for the things you do. Let people see your abilities. Deal directly with other people whenever you can – rather than letting your boss take all the credit. If he is lazy and incompetent, you'll find this easy – he'll be delighted to let you have as much responsibility as you want because it will leave him with less to do. And he'll probably be too stupid to realise that you're carving your way into his territory.

⚭ Early on in your relationship try to get your boss to outline your specific responsibilities. Then tell him how you plan to satisfy those responsibilities. Get his support and agreement for any new or innovative changes.

How to deal with aggressive people

How should you cope when you come face to face with someone who threatens you physically?

Your response will have a significant effect on the outcome! If you act in the wrong way then you will increase your chance of suffering a physical injury!

Here is my advice:

▲ Do not show your potential assailant that you are frightened. If you show fear, the would-be assailant will feel stronger and more powerful. He will be more – not less – likely to hit you.

▲ Try to show him that you are not a threat to him. Keep your voice quiet and calm. Try to look cool and relaxed. If you threaten – and push him into a corner – then you will make him more aggressive.

▲ Try to get him – and everyone else present – to sit down. People are far less aggressive and far less likely to become violent when they are sitting than when they are standing.

▲ If there is a door out of the room do not block it. It is important that you don't block his means of escape. Any assailant will feel nervous, threatened and anxious. If you trap him (even accidentally) he will feel more frightened than ever. As a result he will be more likely to behave violently.

▲ Encourage him to talk to you. It doesn't matter what he talks about. If he feels angry about some political injustice then encourage him to tell you about it. If he feels hatred towards some individual or group then let him get it off his chest. Listen to him when he talks. Offer encouragement. Nod your head and show him that you are listening attentively. If you show him that you are sympathetic – and that you care – then he will be less likely to be violent towards you.

▲ If he is prepared to listen to you, offer him advice and suggestions about ways in which he can deal with his problem. Be his friend. He is probably lonely and frightened. Try to offer him options and alternatives.

▲ When you talk do so in a gentle voice. Never threaten or command. He probably hates figures of authority. He probably needs love and companionship and friendship. Don't be bossy or arrogant. Remember that he is frightened and that you are probably the only person who can calm him down and appease his feeling of anxiety.

▲ Do not show that you expect an attack. Do not shy away from him. Do not remind him that he is expected to be violent. Try to treat him as a normal individual. Try to treat the situation – however strange and abnormal – as entirely normal.

▲ When you are talking open your hands towards him – that simple gesture will help to make him feel more comfortable and more relaxed.

▲ Don't look straight into his eyes and try to stare him down. You'll make him feel more uncomfortable and more threatened if you do. Look at his face or chest but try to keep your eyes away from his eyes.

▲ Don't, whatever you do, argue with him. Don't turn your back on him. Don't push him around. If you do any of these things you will be more likely to push him into attacking you.

▲ Try not to show any emotions. When he makes statements or assertions just show him that you are listening. Don't try to win him over by making aggressive statements of your own. There is a real chance that you will annoy him. He may change his mind and then you will be left stranded.

▲ Keep your muscles relaxed. Try to make your body feel loose rather than tense.

▲ Don't corner him physically or psychologically. Leave him plenty of room to 'escape' – both physically and psychologically. Don't be clever. Don't try to trap him. Wild animals fight much harder and much more aggressively when they are trapped. The human assailant has much in common with a wild animal.

▲ If you are both standing (and you haven't managed to get him to sit down) then try to keep slightly more than an arm's length distance between you. Stand slightly on his weak side too (so, for example, if he is left handed then stand slightly on his right side).

▲ Be polite. However repulsive he may be and however much you may despise him or hate him try to be polite.

Never raise your voice. Listen carefully to what he has to say. Try to learn from every word he utters. When he is talking never interrupt until he's stopped.

How to get power over people

If you have a position of authority, it is easy to exert power over people who are less important than you are – people who work for you, for example. Calling an underling to your office, for example, shows immediately that you are the boss. It leaves little room for misunderstanding. Shouting at someone who cannot shout back requires no sense of style and no understanding of what makes people tick. Wearing a uniform of any kind – even a white coat – gives you an easy and immediate power over people around you. Making people wait for you or making them fill in forms before you will see them makes you seem more important than they are.

It is, however, perfectly possible to exert power over people without having any official or basic authority and without having any real status. You can obtain power over people by the way that you act, the way you speak and the way you move. By using simple 'power play' techniques it is possible to exert power over strangers and business colleagues simply, effectively and efficiently.

Here are some of the ways in which you can get power over people.

☑ Always move with certainty, ease and confidence. If you drive your car into an official car park where you have no right to park the attendant will probably throw you out. If you shout at him he'll shout back. Because he has more authority than you have he will win. He can fetch the security guards or the police and have you forcibly removed. You'll end up losing time and face. If, on the other hand, you drive into the car park and tell the attendant that you are just leaving your car there for a few moments while you pop into the office he will be confused and uncertain. You don't need to lie to him but your very demeanour will suggest to him that you have a right to be there. And he will find it far more difficult to stop you leaving your car. You won't always win – but you will stand a better chance of winning.

☑ If you have your own office you can obtain power over visitors by arranging your furniture in the right way. Make sure, for example, that you have a high backed chair that swivels, has arm rests and can easily be moved in all directions. Make sure, too, that your chair is a little higher than usual. To give yourself immediate power over all visitors make sure that the only chair readily available to visitors is lower and has no arm rests, no castors and no swivel facility. When you are both sitting down you will be in an immediate position of power and authority. If you arrange for your visitors to sit on a low sofa then you'll be in an even greater position of power. I know of one man who had a couple of centimetres shaved off the front legs of the chair his visitors use. The result is that his visitors always feel themselves sliding forwards. They feel slightly uncomfortable – but aren't sure why – and consequently they don't stay too long.

☑ When you are dealing with individuals who work for large organisations, always make sure that you know the name of the person you are dealing with. If you allow people to remain nameless then you will be confronting the whole organisation. If you make sure that you know the name and position of the person you are talking to you will reduce his sense of power and security enormously. He will not be representing the whole organisation any more – he will be speaking for himself and his small part of the organisation. He will, indeed, be vulnerable. If you want to frighten him or subdue him you only have to write down his name, his department and ask him for the name of his superiors. The power will then be in your hands.

☑ If you are prepared to take risks then you've got power over anyone who isn't prepared to take risks. Be prepared to consider the unusual, to create options and alternatives, and you'll have power over people who are content to play everything according to the rules.

People who do not like taking risks will be frightened by you. Their fears give you power.

☑ If you want to obtain power over a particular individual then find out who already has power over that individual. If you can then influence those people – or you can successfully suggest that you have any influence over those people – then you have the power you need. If you are negotiating with a man who thinks his boss owes you a favour then the negotiations will be easy to manipulate in your favour.

☑ Use the power of 'territory' to exert power over the people you meet. If you go into another man's office you will be on 'his' territory. Theoretically, he will be in control. He will have the power. He may, for example, have the high backed, swivel chair while you have the ordinary, cheap, plastic chair to sit on.

But you can, within seconds, take over his territory, make him feel desperately uncomfortable, and win all the power you need.

To begin with move your chair. Never sit on a chair that has been positioned by someone else. If you do then you are sitting somewhere that he wants you to sit. Move the chair around to the side of his desk. The desk is 'his' property. It is 'his' defensive barrier. By moving your chair so that the desk is not directly between you, you will have reduced his power dramatically.

Next, take control of the desk.

You can do this easily by leaning on the desk or by putting your briefcase or papers on the desk. The man who owns the desk will feel uncomfortable and threatened. He will probably sway backwards in his chair. You are now invading his private territory.

You can make your position even stronger – and his even weaker – by moving some of his items on the desk to one side to give you more room. Move his telephone, for example. Maybe put it on the floor out of his reach. Move some of his papers. Move the photo of his wife and children. Move the stapler and the small dictating machine. Slowly the desk becomes your territory. You then have the power.

If you really want to rub home your victory you can sit on his desk – maybe so that you can show him some papers you want him to look at. Or you can stand up and lean on his desk so that he has to look up at you.

If you have a meeting in a restaurant you can use simpler techniques to make sure that you obtain control of the dining table – in order to give you the power. Start, even before you sit down, by selecting your table carefully. Choose a table where your dining partner can sit with his back to the rest of the restaurant. He'll feel uncomfortable. We all feel more relaxed when we have our backs to the wall. (Of course, if you want him to feel relaxed then you should do the opposite – and make sure that he does have his back to the wall.)

Try too to make sure that he can't see anything very much apart from you. Sit in a booth if possible. You don't want him to be distracted or 'saved' at some crucial moment by a distraction or a chance meeting. If possible choose somewhere with dim lighting and quiet, relaxing background music – both these will relax him a little.

Once you're sitting at the table you must make it clear right from the start that you are in control. You should talk to the waiter. You should joke with the wine waiter.

Within seconds of sitting down start to rearrange the table. In the centre of the table there will probably be a flower vase, an ashtray or salt and pepper shakers. These items usually mark the division between your territory and his territory. Make an aggressive, power play move by subtly shifting these items into his half of the table. You can do it idly – as though you were merely fiddling uncomfortably with them. You can do it to make room to put your menu down flat on the table (leaving him having to hold his menu defensively in front of his chest) or you can do it to make room for some essential papers that you want him to look at or sign before the meal is over.

Before you start eating – and before you start negotiating – you will have established that you have the power. He will feel edgy, uncomfortable and slightly frightened of you. He will not be willing to contradict you, argue with you or deny you whatever you want. You will already be close to victory.

☑ Get your timing right. Try to pick your moment carefully. Remember that anticipation is nearly always better than reality. Hookers and travel agents get their customers to pay before they enjoy – rather than afterwards.

☑ Never be afraid to say if you don't understand something. Ask for his help and advice if you like. You'll be turning a competitive situation into a collaborative one. Your confusion will win you sympathy. He'll feel bad about taking advantage of you. He'll be besieged by guilt if he tries to trick you.

☑ Never, ever give an ultimatum unless you're prepared to see it through. Nothing loses you power more than making an ultimatum and then backing down. Remember, however, that if the other person really believes that you are prepared to back up your ultimatum then you probably won't have to.

☑ Remember that when you are using the telephone the caller is always at an advantage. He knew he was calling you before you did. That gives him an edge. He is bound to be better prepared than you are. If you want to regain power then tell him that you'll have to call him back. Plead illness, a caller or simply hang up while you're talking and blame a bad connection afterwards. Remember, too, that it is much easier to say 'no' on the telephone than it is to say 'no' face to face.

☑ If someone comes to your office you can make him feel uncomfortable by leaving the moment he arrives – and leaving him alone. He'll want to look on your desk but he'll feel shy about doing so and being caught. He'll feel slightly edgy, a little annoyed and rather embarrassed. You'll have won an initial power play. If this happens to you then you can regain the initiative by busying yourself with the crossword in a posh newspaper. Make sure you know the answer to a tricky clue before you start this power play! When your host returns to his office let him see that you've been keeping busy with the crossword and ask him if he can help you with the answer to 17 down (or whatever). Read out the clue. Then, before he has a chance to answer, you tell him the solution – which has come to you in a flash of inspiration. He'll probably feel a mixture of relief, embarrassment and admiration.

If you are left to cool your heels in someone else's office the other alternative is to busy yourself with some work and then ask him to wait for just a moment or two while you finish off something that you're doing when he returns.

☑ If you think that a meeting may be boring or difficult to end, fix yourself up some pre-arranged escape routes. Arrange for someone to telephone you at various times. If things are going well you can either ignore the calls or tell the caller to wait. (This will make your visitor feel good because you're making other people wait while you deal with him.) If things are going badly you can use one of these calls as an excuse to end your meeting.

☑ Think carefully before fixing the time for a meeting. If you have to do something that you want to be over as quickly as possible fix the meeting for a few minutes before you have a luncheon appointment – and make it clear from the start that you aren't inviting your visitor to lunch! You will have a cast iron excuse for rushing off as soon as your business is completed. If you have to fire someone, for example, always do it just a few minutes before you have an unbreakable luncheon appointment.

☑ Before any meeting go through all the possible scenarios and problems. If you know the possible dangers – and the answers – then you have the power.

☑ If you want to worry someone at a meeting (and worrying someone is an excellent way to obtain power over him) then take copious notes. Do lots of underlining and put lots of exclamation marks on your notes. The person you're trying to worry will probably spend half the meeting trying to work out what you've written down – and what comments you've made. He'll be convinced that you've noticed things that he has missed.

☑ Ask yourself what is the worst that can happen. Knowing that you can cope with the 'worst' (and the worst is not usually as bad as you think it might be) always gives you a little extra confidence.

☑ Remember: power is very much in the mind. If you think you've got power then you've got power!

☑ Learn how to control the opening of a conversation. If you want to get someone to talk lean backwards, show the palms of your hands, and smile. If you are expansive and appear open and friendly then the person you're talking to will confide in you and share secrets with you.

☑ To end a conversation lean forwards slightly, stand up or merely change your position. Change the tone of your voice, speak a little more loudly or hold out your hand for the other person to shake. All these are usually accepted as clear signs that a meeting is over.

☑ If you really want to take power over someone then invade his 'personal space'. Move forwards and lean closer. The person you want to take power over will lean backwards in order to keep you out of his private space. He will feel uncomfortable, edgy and defensive. I once saw a celebrity use this trick on a television interviewer who was planning to give him a hard time. The celebrity, a skilled television performer, moved very close to the interviewer so that his face was just a few inches from hers. The interviewer who had, just a few moments before, been aggressive and full of confidence, suddenly became nervous and rather frightened. She virtually dried up – allowing the celebrity to dominate the interview completely.

☑ If you want to dominate someone with whom you are doing business – and whom you are meeting at his office – arrange to have messages sent to his office. Then when his secretary brings you the messages ask her to call one or two people on your behalf. Smile at her and give her simple but polite instructions. Suddenly, instead of being a stranger in a man's office you'll be using his office and his secretary to conduct your business. You'll have complete power over him.

☑ Have you ever sat in a room with a group of friends or relatives when one of them has suddenly started yawning? If you have then you'll know that within seconds of one person starting to yawn everyone else will be doing it too. Or have you noticed what happens when the conversation gets round to fleas and someone starts scratching? Within seconds everyone else will be scratching too.

There are several reasons why we mimic one another's behaviour in this way. But one important explanation is that because we all desperately want to be part of a group and want to be liked and accepted, we all tend to adopt the same postures and movements as the people who are close to us. Watch two young lovers sitting on a park bench and you'll notice that if he crosses his legs then she'll cross her legs too. Watch a couple having a meal together. If she leans forward and puts her elbows on the table then (if he likes her and wants to get on with her and wants her to know that he likes her) he'll put his elbows on the table too.

Conscious of what we're doing or not, we all do this all the time. It is our way of passing messages to one another. It is our way of expressing sympathy and agreement. And our way of making friends. But once you are aware that this phenomenon exists it is perfectly possible to use it to your advantage. You can use simple behavioural patterns to help yourself manipulate other people so that they end up liking you or doing what you want them to do.

So, for example, if you want to make someone like you and enjoy your company, you should smile at them as often as you can. A smile makes people feel warm, wanted and loved. The person who sees you smile will respond by smiling back. And because his face is smiling he'll feel happy inside. He won't really know why but he'll like you. And he'll want to see you again.

If you are a salesman, you can use this technique to help yourself improve your sales record. If you appear on someone's doorstep trying to sell encyclopaedias and you frown at them all the time then your potential customers will feel uncomfortable and unhappy. They won't like you very much. And they'll probably say 'no' to your product. Appear on someone's doorstep with your encyclopaedias and a smile and you'll be much more likely to make a sale. Incidentally, this works the other way round too. If someone is trying to sell you something and you want to say 'no' without hurting his feelings too much then smile at him. He won't feel so bad when he goes away empty handed.

In just the same way that you can manipulate people by smiling at them, so you can manipulate people by the way you use your body. If you want to relax someone then make sure that your own body looks relaxed.

If you have difficulty in meeting people or making new friends, you may well be frightening people off by appearing too cold. You may just feel shy but that shyness may come across as 'coolness' and may make people feel that if they try talking to you then they risk humiliation or rejection. Learn to smile and to relax your body and you'll soon find that strangers smile and relax when they're with you.

How to avoid being manipulated

Before any negotiations start you should be aware that your opponent may be trying to use your weaknesses against you. You should be aware that mental strengths and weaknesses are as important at the negotiating table as physical strengths and weaknesses are in the boxing ring. If you are to win then you must know yourself.

To help yourself understand your motives, ambitions and weaknesses more comprehensively I suggest that you look through the section entitled 'How To Understand Other People' and apply the comments to yourself. You will also benefit by reading my book *Know Yourself*.

How to make people like you

♥ Be a good listener. People love talking about themselves. But remember that there is more to being a good listener than just being silent – furniture is silent! Nod your head while they're talking. Listen carefully to what they are saying. And ask questions that show you've been listening.

♥ Learn to flatter people carefully and subtly. Say things like 'I've never looked at it like that before – but you're right' or 'I agree with what you've said but I've never been able to put it as succinctly as that'. Make the person you are talking to feel that he is special and talented. The more you manage to convince him that you mean it the more he'll like you.

♥ Get people to help you in small ways that won't cost them much time, effort or money. Most people get a warm glow inside them if they help someone. If a woman asks a man to help her with her suitcase then the man will feel good about it! He'll like the woman he's helped because she's made him feel pleased with himself.

♥ Smile at them. To see just how effective this is, smile at someone every time he uses a particular word. You'll discover that he will unconsciously use that particular word more and more often. He'll be getting an appreciative response from you and he'll respond accordingly. He won't know why he is doing it but he'll want to please you, and see you smile, and so he'll keep on doing it. Similarly, if you smile at someone every time he does something you want him to keep on doing you'll find that he keeps repeating the action. He may not know why he is doing it and he may not even know that he is repeating himself. But he'll keep on because it feels good. The evidence shows that the more you smile at someone (within obvious limits) the more he will like you and want to do things for you.

How to deal with people who try to embarrass you

If someone deliberately tries to embarrass you, it's a fairly safe bet that he is fairly easy to embarrass. So, if someone tries to embarrass you by saying something rude or telling a rude joke turn the tables on him by, for example, saying 'I don't understand – would you please explain that to me.'

Theory into Practice

• • • • • • • • • • • • • • • • • • • •

Now that you've learnt how to watch people accurately and successfully you'll be able to use your new skills in a wide variety of situations.

You will be able to use your skills to help you make remarkably accurate judgements about the people you know and the strangers you meet. You'll be able to entertain yourself while waiting for trains or planes by 'reading' your fellow passengers.

And you will, of course, be able to use your new skills to manipulate people who would normally have a lot of control over you.

So, for example, imagine that you're visiting your bank manager. When you walk into his office he will be sitting behind a desk. The desk will help to defend his personal space. And it will give him status and authority. But you can 'capture' the desk and use it to your own advantage.

You must take charge as soon as you get into his office.

Walk straight across to his desk – as confidently as you can – and put your bag, briefcase or hat down on top of it. If there is a chair sitting waiting for you then move it so that you can rest your arms and body down on the desk. When the preliminaries are over take out a notepad and pen and place both on the desk in front of you.

Within seconds of entering the bank manager's office you will have 'taken over' his desk. You will have the authority and the strength. He will suddenly feel nervous and apprehensive. The normal relationship between bank manager and client will have been reversed.

You can use exactly the same technique when you go to visit your doctor for doctors use desks to establish their authority too. When you visit the surgery and your doctor waves you to a chair a couple of feet in front of his desk he is putting you in an exposed and vulnerable situation. He possesses the desk and is defended by its bulk. You sit alone with your personal space unprotected.

But it is very easy to reverse the situation and take control.

When you enter the surgery move the chair a few inches so that it is closer to the desk. Then sit down so that you can lean forwards and put your elbows on the desk. If there is a letter rack in front of you then gently but firmly move it to one side. Put your hat, gloves, newspaper, shopping or note-book down on the desk.

If your doctor is leaning forwards then he will almost certainly respond by leaning backwards and abandoning his territorial control. His response will be automatic. You will then be able to start your consultation in a much stronger position.

You will, I am sure, be able to think of hundreds of other situations in which you can put the information and advice you have gleaned from this book to good use!

Published by the European Medical Journal

The Traditional Home Doctor

Vernon Coleman

Packed with practical health tips

Contents include:

•• and much, much more! ••

ISBN 0 9521492 7 3   232pp   £9.95

Published by the European Medical Journal

Food for Thought

Your guide to healthy eating

Vernon Coleman

Packed with easy-to-use, up to date, practical information, *Food for Thought* is designed to help you differentiate between fact and fantasy when planning your diet. The book's 28 chapters include:

- Food the fuel: basic information about carbohydrates, protein, fat, vitamins and minerals
- When water isn't safe to drink—and what to do about it
- How what you eat affects your health
- Why snacking is good for you
- The mini-meal diet and the painless way to lose weight
- Quick tips for losing weight
- The Thirty-Nine Steps to Slenderness
- 20 magic superfoods that can improve your health
- The harm food additives can do
- 20-point plan for avoiding food poisoning
- Drugs and hormones in food
- Food irradiation, genetically altered food, microwaves
- 30 common diseases—and their relationship to what you eat
- How to eat a healthy diet
- 21 reasons for being a vegetarian
- How much should you weigh?
- How to deal with children who are overweight

ISBN 0 9521492 6 5
192pp   paperback   £9.95

Published by the European Medical Journal

How to Conquer Pain

A new and positive approach to the problem of persistent and recurrent pain

Vernon Coleman

A fully revised and updated edition of *Natural Pain Control.*
This book tells you

- Factors which influence the amount of pain you feel
- Doctors, drugs and pain control
- How to get the best out of pills
- Alternative therapies that work
- The unique Pain Control Progamme
- How to use your imagination to conquer your pain
- How to sleep when pain is the problem
- The magic of the TENS machine
- Learn how to relax and control your stress
- How to measure your pain
- •• and lots, lots more! ••

What they said about the first edition:
☞ A clear and helpful handbook for pain sufferers… Perhaps most important of all is the way in which it brings pain down to a manageable level and gives self help ideas for sufferers.
The Guardian
☞ Full of good ideas *Mother and Baby*
☞ A new and positive approach *Keep Fit*
☞ An authoritative guide to this universal problem
Bournemouth Evening Echo

ISBN 0 9521492 9 X 192pp paperback £9.95

Published by the European Medical Journal

Bodypower

The secret of self-healing

Vernon Coleman

A new edition of a book that hit the Sunday Times and Bookseller 'Top Ten' charts.

- How your body can heal itself
- How your personality affects your health
- How to use bodypower to stay healthy
- How to stay slim for life
- How to conquer 90% of all illnesses without a doctor
- How to improve your eyesight
- How to fight cancer
- How to use bodypower to help you break bad habits
- How to relax your body and your mind
- How to use bodypower to improve your shape

•• and much, much more! ••

What they said about the first edition:

☞ Don't miss it! Dr Coleman's theories could change your life
Sunday Mirror

☞ If you've got Bodypower, you may never need visit your doctor again, or take another pill! *Slimmer*

☞ A marvellously succint and simple account of how the body can heal itself without resort to drugs *Spectator*

☞ Could make stress a thing of the past *Woman's World*

☞ Shows you how to listen to your body *Woman's Own*

☞ Could help save the NHS from slow strangulation
The Scotsman

ISBN 0 9521492 8 1 160pp paperback £9.95

Published by the European Medical Journal

Mindpower

How to use your mind to heal your body

Vernon Coleman

A new edition of this bestselling manual
- A new approach to health care
- How your mind influences your body
- How to control destructive emotions
- How to deal with guilt
- How to harness positive emotions
- How daydreaming can relax your mind
- How to use your personal strengths
- How to conquer your weaknesses
- How to teach yourself mental self defence
- Specific advice to help you enjoy good health
- •• and much, much more! ••

What they said about the first edition:
☞ Dr Coleman explains the importance of a patient's mental attitude in controlling and treating illness, and suggests some easy-to-learn techniques *Woman's World*
☞ An insight into the most powerful healing agent in the world—the power of the mind *Birmingham Post*
☞ Based on an inspiring message of hope
Western Morning News
☞ It will be another bestseller *Nursing Times*

ISBN 1 898947 00 7
256pp paperback £9.95

Published by the European Medical Journal

Why Animal Experiments Must Stop

And how you can help stop them

Vernon Coleman

"The most damning indictment of vivisection
ever published"

"Essential reading for anyone wishing to counter the
arguments of the vivisectors"

Dr Coleman analyses all the pro-vivisection arguments
one by one—and destroys them.
The moral, ethical, scientific and medical arguments are all
dealt with.

Animal tests can produce dangerously misleading information.
Penicillin kills cats and guinea pigs. Aspirin kills cats.
Digitalis is so toxic to animals that it would never have been
cleared for humans, but it remains our most useful heart drug.
Yet practolol, which was judged safe after animal tests, caused
damage to human patients and had to be withdrawn.

Dr Coleman makes it clear that animal experiments are useless
today and have always been useless.

This book also describes the alternatives to animal experiments.
It offers readers a 10-point plan to help them make sure that
vivisection is stopped, putting an end to one of the
world's most barbaric practices.

ISBN 0 9521492 1 4

128pp   paperback   £9.95

Published by the European Medical Journal

Betrayal of Trust

Vernon Coleman

Betrayal of Trust follows in the tradition of Vernon Coleman's most iconoclastic and ground-breaking books—*The Medicine Men, Paper Doctors,* and *The Health Scandal.*

Dr Coleman catalogues the incompetence and dishonesty of the medical profession and the pharmaceutical industry and explains the historical background to the problems which exist today. He shows how drugs are put onto the market without being properly tested, and provides hard evidence for his astonishing assertion that doctors now do more harm than good.

To support his claim that drug companies use animal tests to get their drugs on the market, Dr Coleman lists scores of widely prescribed drugs which are reguarly prescribed for patients, despite the fact that there is evidence showing that the drugs cause serious problems when given to animals.

Drug companies are, he explains, in a 'no lose' situation. If a new drug seems safe when given to animals, the company making it uses that evidence to help get the drug a licence. But if a new drug causes problems when given to animals, that evidence is ignored as irrelevant! Only patients lose.

"When animal experiments are stopped," says Dr Coleman, "they will never be reintroduced. The moral, ethical, scientific and medical evidence all supports the contention than animal experiments must be stopped now."

ISBN 0 9521492 3 0

160pp paperback £9.95

Also published by the European Medical Journal

Relief from IBS

Simple steps for long-term control

Vernon Coleman

- Causes and symptoms of Irritable Bowel Syndrome
- The two-step control programme
- How you should change your diet
- How to look after your digestive system
- Relief from wind
- Watch out for foods that make your symptoms worse
- Stand up for yourself
- Build up your self-confidence
- Learn to relax your body and mind
- How worrying more can help you worry less
- Tips to help you cope with stress
- Take control of your life

1 898947 03 1
128pp   paperback   £9.95

Also published by the European Medical Journal

Toxic Stress and the Twentieth-Century Blues

Vernon Coleman

Never have I read a book that is so startlingly true. I was dumb-founded by your wisdom. I have long been a fan of your writings. You will go down in history as one of the truly great health reformers of our time.

(Extracted from a letter to the author)

We live in a world which would seem, on the surface, to offer us all the material things we need. Few of us go cold and hungry and the miracles of science and technology surround us – offering us opportunities that our ancestors would have found unbelievable. But underneath this veneer of contentment, society is sicker than ever. Violence and crime against property are increasing; the incidence of mental illness is rising reapidly, the divorce rate is higher than ever with more than 1 in 3 marriages failing. Examine society closely and you will find that sadness, frustration, boredom and fear are rife – and how many of us can honestly claim never to have felt one, if not all, of these emotions on a regular basis?

In this important book, Vernon Coleman examines the underlying causes of the sadness in our society and, most importantly, offers a programme of help and guidance to those who are suffering from 'the twentieth-century blues'. This thought-provoking book reveals many harsh and frightening aspects to the world we live in, but will also help sufferers regain their zest for living by overcoming loneliness, conquering stress and finding new purpose and meaning in life.

1 898947 93 7
107pp   £9.95 paperback

The Bilbury Chronicles

The first in a series of novels following the adventures and exploits of a young GP who begins work in an idyllic Exmoor village

0 9503527 5 6   230pp   £12.95 hardback

Bilbury Grange

The second novel in the series which sees the newly married doctor moving into his new home – a vast, rambling country manor in desparate need of renovation

0 9503527 7 2   247pp   £12.95 hardback

The Bilbury Revels

The third novel in the series sees the village of Bilbury united in a fundraising effort after a devastating storm hist the village

1 0898146 05 5   270pp   £12.95 hardback

Bilbury Pie

A collection of short stories featuring the characters from the Bilbury series of novels

0 8980146 15 2   149pp   £9.95 hardback

The Village Cricket Tour

The story of an amateur cricket team on tour in the West Country

0 9503527 3 X   173pp   £9.95 hardback

The Man Who Inherited a Golf Course

The hero of the story wakes up one morning to find that he has inherited a golf course in his uncle's will

0 9503527 9 9   237pp   £12.95 hardback

Thomas Winsden's Cricketing Almanack

A spoof of the cricketing 'bible', Wisden

1 898146 00 4   128pp   £9.95 hardback

Mrs Caldicott's Cabbage War

A charming story telling of one woman's fight against society and her battle to keep her independence after the death of her husband. A truly inspiring book

0 9503527 8 0   150pp   £9.95 hardback

Deadline

A thriller set in London and Paris and featuring ex-investigative journalist Mark Watson

1 898146 10 1   164pp   £9.95 hardback

All books featured on these pages available from:
Publishing House, Trinity Place, Barnstaple,
Devon EX32 9HJ, England.
Tel: 01271 328892   Fax: 01271 328768
Full catalogue of titles available on request